THE WORLD'S WORST

MILITARY DISASTERS

THE WORLD'S WORST
MILITARY DISASTERS

CHRONICLING THE GREATEST BATTLEFIELD CATASTROPHES OF ALL TIME

CHRIS McNAB

First published in 2005 for Grange Books
An imprint of Grange Books Ltd
35 Riverside
Sir Thomas Longley Road
Medway City Estate
Rochester, Kent
ME2 4DP
www.grangebooks.co.uk

A catalogue record for this book is available from
the British Library.

ISBN-10: 1-84013-808-4
ISBN-13: 978-1-84013-808-5

Editorial and design by
Amber Books Ltd
Bradley's Close
74–77 White Lion Street
London N1 9PF
www.amberbooks.co.uk

Project Editor: Sarah Uttridge
Picture Researcher: Terry Forshaw
Design: EQ Media

Printed in Thailand

CONTENTS

INTRODUCTION

IN WAR, IT IS AN OBVIOUS POINT THAT ONE SIDE'S DISASTER USUALLY IMPLIES THE OTHER SIDE'S TRIUMPH. THE COLLAPSE OF FRENCH FORCES AT DIEN BIEN PHU IN 1954, FOR EXAMPLE, WAS THE CATASTROPHIC RESULT OF STRATEGIC AND TACTICAL OVERREACH ON THE PART OF THE FRENCH.

Their commanders isolated 15,000 French soldiers in Dien Bien Phu valley at the end of a tenuous air supply and chronically underestimated the forces arraigned against them. The results of these decisions are now well known to history – a five-month siege leading to the deaths of more than 7000 French troops and the surrender of an additional 12,000.

When one side suffers a disaster, however, it can tend to overshadow the achievements of the opposing side who secured victory. Vo Nguyen Giap's campaign at Dien Bien Phu, although characteristically dismissive of casualties (the Viet Minh lost more than 20,000 men during the siege), was characterized by the daring and ruthless persistence that wins battles. Through incredible logistical feats, which allowed Giap to ring the French with field and anti-aircraft artillery in the surrounding mountains, and by adapting to the failure of initial mass assaults, Giap steadily wore down an enemy supposedly his technological and tactical superior. In other words, there would have been no French disaster at Dien Bien Phu were it not for the astounding talents of the enemy.

THE INGREDIENTS OF DISASTER

The simple reminder not to overlook the victor's achievements in preference for the defeated's failings gives us the first ingredient of what constitutes such disasters – successful enemy action. This is far from the sum total of military failure, and indeed it is awkward to create a definitive list of the qualities shared by all military disasters. Obviously, military disaster is never a simple matter of having greater casualties than the enemy – as Dien Bien Phu proved. More disproportionately, the US Special Forces action in Mogadishu in 1993 is rightly considered a military disaster, yet is set against the fact that US troops killed up to 1000 enemy troops for the loss of 18 dead.

The Mogadishu example also proves that a military disaster is not necessarily defined by enormous loss of life. History has a bloody catalogue of battles where blood has been spilt in torrents, many of which are in this book, but the loss of 70 men is just as catastrophic for a company as the loss of 1000 men for a division. The SAS's infamous Bravo Two Zero operation in Iraq in 1991 resulted in just three dead and four

➥

captured, but such was an attrition rate of 90 per cent in a patrol of just eight men.

If we were to define the single most important ingredient in a military disaster, it might be chronic mission failure. After all, a disaster is not truly a disaster if the original objectives are achieved. In this book, offensive and defensive plans not only hit problems, but also completely and devastatingly unravel. To choose a famous example, the Spanish Armada set sail in May 1588 with the intention of supporting the Spanish Army of Flanders in making a successful invasion of England. However, not only was the invasion never attempted, but also the Spanish lost 70 vessels out of 130 and suffered 15,000 dead for absolutely no significant tactical or attritional successes against the enemy. Similarly, in September 1812 the renowned Duke of Wellington lay siege to the French-occupied walled fortress city of Burgos in Castille during the Peninsular War. A month later Wellington withdrew his troops, the fortress still in French hands and his own troops having suffered some 2000 dead in a series of futile, incompetent and ill-conceived battles.

In addition to mission failure as an ingredient of military disaster, we might also add, less securely, the total degeneration of a force's command and control structures. The moment when officers lose control of their force is the moment when a threat of defeat can turn into a hideous rout. At Marathon in 490 BC, the Persians found themselves trapped in an expertly handled pincer movement by the Athenians.

Despite outnumbering the Athenians three-to-one, the Persians lost all sense of tactical response, resulting in a panicked flight back to their ships. The consequences of this were 6400 Persian dead against 194 Athenian fatalities, a disproportionate casualty count that cannot be explained purely by the excellence of the Athenian tactics, but must also take into consideration the loss of Persian cohesion.

Marathon illustrates another quality of some of the greatest military disasters, in which the defeat in a single battle means the loss of the entire campaign or war. Taking an aerial view of history, the significance of Hitler's defeat at Stalingrad in the winter of 1942–43 was not purely the loss of the entire German Sixth Army, a loss Hitler could not afford, but arguably the beginning of the total German defeat in World War II. After Stalingrad, the German war essentially became a defensive one, the Wehrmacht beginning a hideously costly two-year retreat back into the Reich, leading to ultimate defeat. Stalingrad as a military disaster was not simply confined to the banks of the Volga, but had a direct influence on the cataclysmic battle for Berlin in 1945.

CAUSES

While there may be some common ingredients to military disasters, the actual causes vary a great deal. Many military disasters are traceable to an instance of human error.

➤➤

For example, Lieutenant Colonel Alexander Thorneycroft failed to enforce the proper creation of defensive positions atop Spion Kop on the night of 23 January 1900, and as a consequence 650 of his 1700-strong force were slaughtered by Boer gunfire the next day. Another example from the annals of the British Army would be Major General William Elphinstone's fateful decision in Afghanistan in 1842 to march 16,500 soldiers and civilians from Kabul to Jelalabad, a distance of 130km (80 miles) passing entirely through mountainous rebel-held territory. Only one man reached safety.

HUMAN ERROR

Human error in battle is not uniform in type. Sometimes it is caused by arrogance, by carelessness, by lack of training or by simply being outclassed by the enemy (as many of Napoleon's opponents discovered). Sometimes the error is not on the part of battlefield leaders, but belongs to support services, particularly intelligence. A sloppy treatment of information from communications intercepts, spy sources and radar signals contributed to the total lack of US preparedness at Pearl Harbor in December 1941. Likewise, the Allied dismissal of intelligence reports from around Arnhem in 1944 aided the disastrous failure of Montgomery's Operation Market Garden. On other occasions the disaster occurs not entirely from battlefield decision, but from technological disadvantage as well. The French defeat at Agincourt in 1415 was substantially caused by a lack of French answer to the hails of arrows from Henry's talented archers, the English advantage in firepower outweighing the French three-to-one advantage in numbers. In sixteenth-century Japan, at the battle of Nagashino (1575), the samurai warriors of Takeda Katsuyori – some of the most highly trained soldiers in the medieval world – were decimated by matchlock fire from men with a fraction of the military expertise. Leaping ahead to the twentieth century, the battlefields of the Western Front were soaked heavily in the blood of those men cut down by Maxim or Vickers machine guns, weapons which brought the processes of industry into the business of killing.

ADVANCED TECHNOLOGY

Military disasters caused by technology frequently occur at those junctures in history when new weapons technologies emerge on the battlefield, the period of adjustment to the changed killing environment usually being a slaughterous one. However, there are some other factors more constant throughout history, the weather being the classic spoiler of military plans. The landscape and climate of Russia, for instance, has been destroying armies for hundreds of years. Napoleon's 600,000-strong French army was decimated in 1812 by the Russian winter, and Hitler's armies had a similar experience

➤➤

in the 1940s. In 1281, a Mongol army – 150,000 men – attempted an amphibious invasion of Japan. A massive typhoon wrecked the Mongol fleet, killing around 100,000 men and preventing the Japanese occupation.

Logistics

While the Mongol disaster seems to have resided entirely in the lap of the gods, the failure of Napoleon and Hitler to handle the Russian winter was compounded by deficiencies in arguably the most crucial element of any military campaign – logistics. The relationship between the logistical train and combat troops has been likened to the relationship between a spear tip and the spear shaft. A commander's fighting troops may be the best in the business, but if they are not properly and constantly fed, watered, armed, sheltered and rested, then their ability to wage war will eventually collapse. Many of the disasters mentioned – Dien Bien Phu and Stalingrad, – have featured logistical failure as a critical, sometimes deciding, factor in their outcomes. Conversely, some armies can be formidably well supplied and still fall apart in battle. The US Army in Korea in 1950 had vast supplies of equipment, but was routed by the Chinese in the communist October campaign.

THINKING ON DISASTER

There are many different causes of military disaster, whatever these causes may be there is no doubt at all that they are a truly fascinating historical phenomena to study, illustrating the heights and depth of human behaviour and military outcomes. However, here lies a danger. Many of the battles discussed in this book are very well known and discussed often, battles which are familiar tend to lose the personal sense of tragedy that should be theirs. A Roman soldier fighting in, say, the Teutoburg forest in AD 9 would have absolutely no idea that his imminent slaughter at the hands of the Germanic enemy would become the subject of historical fascination. For him, his last moments would unfortunately be limited to the individual terror of death, and the deaths of 20,000 of his comrades would not reduce the significance of that event for his family and loved ones.

A military disaster consists of thousands of horrific individual disasters, thousands of stopped heartbeats. To remember this gives us a much better insight into the true nature of military disaster, and prevents us regarding such events as nothing more than board-game history.

ANCIENT BATTLES
2000 BC – 300 BC

The armies and technologies involved in military disasters may change over the centuries, but the essential causes of incompetence, misjudgement, logistical failure and freak event have remained constant. In the earliest days of recorded history, we see military catastrophes strike suddenly in the midst of a confident campaign. At Kadesh (c.1274 BC), Mutawalli's ambush of Egyptian troops turned into the encirclement and destruction of his own forces, and at Marathon (490 BC) more than 6000 Persians were killed for the loss of fewer than 200 Athenians, despite the Persians' huge numerical advantage. Such battles illustrate the rapid slip from impending victory to devastating rout.

Left: The battle of Salamis in 480 BC where at least 200
Persian vessels were sunk.

BATTLE OF MEGIDDO

THE BATTLE OF MEGIDDO IS ONE OF THE FIRST BATTLES IN HISTORY TO BE PROPERLY RECORDED, DETAILS OF THE ACTION COMING MAINLY FROM EGYPTIAN TEMPLE INSCRIPTIONS.

Taking place *circa* 1479 BC, it was fought around the city of Tel Megiddo in Palestine and was a clash between the Egyptian army of Thutmosis III and an assortment of rebel Canaanite cities directed by the kings of Kadesh and Megiddo. The area was politically contentious, dominating as it did trade routes between Egypt and Mesopotamia, so when the Canaanites rose up against Egypt, Thutmosis marched 10,000 men from Sileh on the Egyptian border to Yaham on the edge of rebel territory.

REBEL STRATEGY
Megiddo was to prove a disaster for the rebels, although at first they appeared to be well deployed and militarily strong. Two blocks of rebel infantry were positioned near Yokneam and Taanakh – to the east and west of Megiddo, respectively – while Palestinian charioteers were concealed around the city itself, on the Plain of Esdraelon. The rebel plan was to allow the ➤➤

KEY FACTS

***c.*1479 BC** – Canaanite tribes rebel against the regional authority of Egypt and draw the Egyptians into battle around Megiddo in Palestine.

Canaanite strategy overturned by unexpected route of travel chosen by Egyptians.

Canaanites collapse under three-winged Egyptian attack, and Megiddo falls after a long siege.

Palestine in the second millennnium BC *was an environment suited to cavalry and infantry warfare. Cities and towns were generally circumscribed by flatlands ideal for the fast movement of mounted formations and for massed infantry charges.*

Egyptians to attack the infantry, who would then feign retreat and lure the Egyptians to break ranks and expose their flanks to a sudden attack by the chariots. However, a wise decision by Thutmosis meant that his army advanced along a difficult central route to the battlefield across a narrow highland path, rather than taking easier but less secure routes through Yokneam and Taanakh.

COLLAPSE

The Canaanites were thrown into disarray by the unexpected positions of the enemy and had to redeploy to protect Megiddo itself. The redeployment failed – and the next day, the Canaanites found themselves faced by a massive three-wing enveloping attack from the Egyptians. Despite having vast armies at their disposal, the Canaanites were outmanoeuvred, and crumbled. Primary sources give the impression of a mindless rout as Egyptian chariots, infantry and archers slaughtered the fleeing troops. The inhabitants of Megiddo were so terrified of the Egyptians that they refused to open the city gates for the survivors – the desperate soldiers were forced to climb over the walls using knotted sheets. Megiddo was placed under siege by the Egyptians, and the city finally fell after seven months. The Canaanites had paid terribly for their rebellion. ■

Egyptian chariots had considerable advantages of speed on the ancient battlefield, and so were generally used for flanking and shock attacks.

Cities in the ancient Middle East could be formidable defensive works. They often consisted of outer walls surrounded by a ditch, with tower structures providing observation posts and archery platforms.

KADESH

**DURING THE SECOND MILLENNIUM BC, THE HITTITE EMPIRES'
MAJOR OPPONENT IN THE MIDDLE EAST WAS EGYPT, RULED BY
PHARAOH RAMSES II (1304–1237 BC).**

Around 1274 BC, a Hittite army under king Mutawalli closed
with Ramses' Egyptians around Kadesh, a city in Canaan situated
on the Orontes River.

MUTAWALLI'S STRATEGY

Mutawalli had a force of 3000 chariots and around 20,000
infantry; the Egyptians amassed roughly 2000 chariots and
16,000 infantry. Mutawalli's strategy was one of ambush and
disinformation. As Ramses marched north towards Kadesh with
four divisions, two Bedouin in Mutawalli's employ told him that
the Hittites were much further north at Aleppo. Consequently,
Ramses split his forces, taking two divisions across the Orontes
while leaving the remainder behind the river.

   Meanwhile, Mutawalli waited with his forces to the northwest
of Kadesh, a city where Ramses and his Amon division made
camp, ignorant of the threat. However, two Hittite scouts were ➤➤

KEY FACTS

c.1274 BC – Hittites
successfully split Egyptian
forces through the use of
disinformation, before
attacking them around
Kadesh, Canaan.

Egyptians under Ramses II
manage to fight off collapse,
and hold on long enough for
reinforcements to arrive.

Hittite army is destroyed,
despite being numerically
superior to its enemy.

Egypt was capable of martialling a professional army as far back as the late third millennium, when a professional militia could be recruited from Egyptian tribes and trained through a formalized process of instruction.

captured and tortured into confessing the true location of the Hittite troops.

RAMSES RALLIES HIS MEN

Messages were sent for the rearguard divisions to close up, but before they could do so the Hittites launched a two-pronged attack. The camp was soon the scene of murderous fighting, with Egyptian forces splitting and panicking. Yet Ramses rallied his men, and used archers to regain some battlefield control. He swung a portion of his army into the right flank of the Hittites, pushing them back against the Orontes. At the same time, other Egyptian divisions arrived, having received news of the attack. The Hittites were steadily encircled, despite Mutawalli committing another 1000 chariots to the battle. The Hittites were crushed. Having first lost the element of surprise, the Hittites had been outclassed by Egyptian military skill and lost thousands of men. ■

Above: The two-wheeled chariot developed in the Middle East around 1700 BC. Both driver and archer underwent up to three years of training to become an integrated fighting team. Right: An aerial map illustrating the battle of Kadesh.

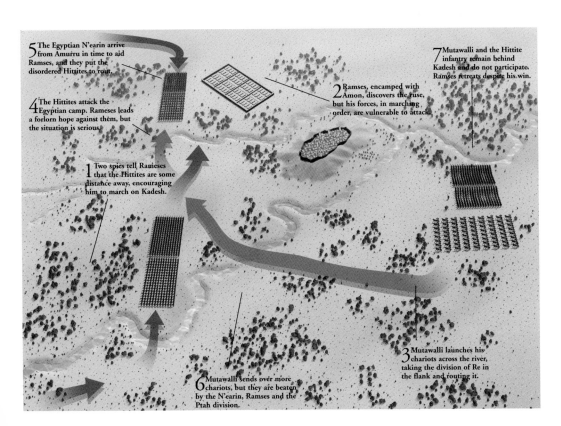

5 The Egyptian N'earin arrive from Amurru in time to aid Ramses, and they put the disordered Hittites to rout.

4 The Hittites attack the Egyptian camp. Rameses leads a forlorn hope against them, but the situation is serious.

1 Two spies tell Rameses that the Hittites are some distance away, encouraging him to march on Kadesh.

2 Ramses, encamped with Amon, discovers the ruse, but his forces, in marching order, are vulnerable to attack.

7 Mutawalli and the Hittite infantry remain behind Kadesh and do not participate. Ramses retreats despite his win.

3 Mutawalli launches his chariots across the river, taking the division of Re in the flank and routing it.

6 Mutawalli sends over more chariots, but they are beaten by the N'earin, Ramses and the Ptah division.

MARATHON

THE BATTLE OF MARATHON IN 490 BC BROUGHT THE MIGHT OF THE SPREADING PERSIAN EMPIRE INTO CONFLICT WITH THE STATE OF ATHENS.

In August, the Persian king Darius I gathered together an enormous invasion force of 25,000 troops, embarked it aboard 600 vessels, and sent it towards the Greek mainland led by Artaphernes (Darius' nephew) and a noble called Datis. The troops put ashore on the coast of Attica at Marathon, a sheltered anchorage bordered by a large mountain-ringed plain. Athens itself lay only 40km (25 miles) away.

ATTACK THE BEST FORM OF DEFENCE

The Athenians had established blocking defences at the southern end of the plain, and the opposing forces remained static for five days. Datis, however, grew tired of waiting and, leaving a holding force under Artaphernes, embarked cavalry and infantry aboard the ships and slipped away on the night of 11/12 August, with the intention of landing at Phaleron Bay and making a surprise advance on Athens itself. However, the Athenians were ➤➤

A dramatic depiction of the the Greek victory at the battle of Marathon. Typical Greek infantry armaments consisted of a short sword for close-quarters combat and a throwing/stabbing javelin of some 2.5–3.5m (8–11ft) in length.

warned of the plan by spies, and as a consequence launched a massive attack at Marathon.

TACTICAL SUPERIORITY

The Persians outnumbered the Athenians by three-to-one, and the elite Persian troops in the centre were soon pushing back the Athenian centre. However, the Athenian generals Callimarchus and Miltiades had deliberately weakened their own centre, while advancing on the flanks. Before the Persians realized what was happening, they had trapped themselves in a consummate pincer movement. The Persians were now routed, forced to flee back to their ships. Hundreds of Persians drowned during the flight. All survivors had left by 9 a.m., leaving behind 6400 dead for only 192 Athenians killed. The Persian calamity was compounded when Datis approached Athens to find that Miltiades had already deployed a defensive force around the city – he was forced to depart and sail for home. ■

Above: Fragments of ancient Greek weaponry, including a short sword and several javelin and arrow heads. A typical hoplite sword was double-edged, with the blade measuring around 60cm (24in) in length and generally flared out from the hilt.

Right: The map clearly shows the Greek flanking manoeuvre in action.

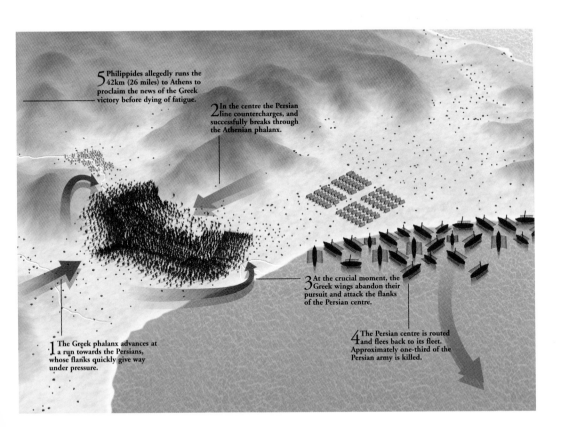

5 Philippides allegedly runs the 42km (26 miles) to Athens to proclaim the news of the Greek victory before dying of fatigue.

2 In the centre the Persian line countercharges, and successfully breaks through the Athenian phalanx.

3 At the crucial moment, the Greek wings abandon their pursuit and attack the flanks of the Persian centre.

1 The Greek phalanx advances at a run towards the Persians, whose flanks quickly give way under pressure.

4 The Persian centre is routed and flees back to its fleet. Approximately one-third of the Persian army is killed.

SALAMIS

THE BATTLE OF SALAMIS WAS ONE OF THE DECIDING BATTLES OF THE GRECO-PERSIAN WARS, AND A GREAT VICTORY FOR THE ATHENIAN GENERAL THEMISTOCLES.

In 480 BC, the Persian navy had a numerical superiority over the Greek fleet, possibly around 1200 vessels compared to the Greeks' 300 or 400. However, the vital Greek advantage lay in their knowledge of the local coastal waters, and it was this knowledge that Themistocles applied to defeat the Persians, along with the skill of the Spartan fleet commander Eurybiades.

OUTMANOEUVRED

Victory at the earlier battle of Thermopylae meant that Persian confidence was riding high when the navy was drawn into battle between the island of Salamis and the coast of Attica. The waters here form a narrow strait, which constricted the front ranks of the Persian vessels, therefore reducing the advantage of numbers. Xerxes, the successor of Darius I, ordered the Persian fleet into the straits (possibly on 28 September). In a fantastic act of hubris, Xerxes set up a throne on the overlooking slopes of Mount ➤➤

> ### KEY FACTS
>
> **480 BC** – Persian fleet of 1200 vessels defeated by around 400 ships of the Greek alliance.
>
> **Persian fleet** is unable to manoeuvre effectively in the narrow strait between Salamis and the coast of Attica.
>
> **Greek fleet** consists of nimble trireme and pentekonter vessels more suited to battle in confined waters.

An artist's representation of the battle of Salamis, depicting a Greek trireme about to ram a Persian vessel. The crucial objective in such ancient naval battles was to attempt to spoil the enemy formations so that the ships' vulnerable flanks were exposed.

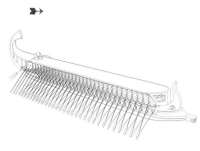

Above: The trireme was Greece's primary fighting vessel by around 500 BC. A typical trireme was around 35m (115ft) in length and featured up to 170 oarsmen, who could power the vessel to around 11.5 knots. Above the rowers was a full fighting deck.

Right: The Persian navy had no room for manoeuvre once it entered the straits.

Aegaleus, to gain a grandstand view of his victory. However, the night before the battle, Xerxes had received disinformation from Themistocles that the Greek ships were attempting an escape – no such attempt was being made, and Xerxes' men would go into battle exhausted from a night of searching.

GREEK TRAP

As the huge Persian fleet entered the straits, Corinthian vessels in the Greek vanguard seemed to flee, drawing the Persians further into the narrow waters. Suddenly, nimble Greek trireme vessels appeared in huge numbers and began ramming the more cumbersome Persian ships, while firing arrows and javelins at the Persian deck crews. Crucially, only around 100 Persian ships could fit in the straits at any one time. These could not manoeuvre effectively in the confines, and were also trapped by the vessels behind them. Xerxes watched the Greeks destroy wave after wave of his fleet, with at least 200 Persian vessels being sunk. The surviving Persians now fled, and Xerxes made an embarrassed journey back to Persia. ■

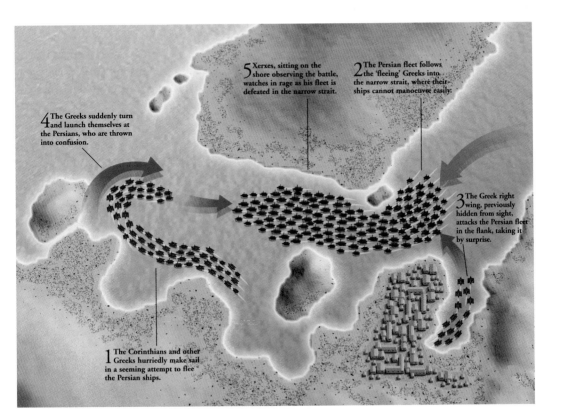

5 Xerxes, sitting on the shore observing the battle, watches in rage as his fleet is defeated in the narrow strait.

2 The Persian fleet follows the 'fleeing' Greeks into the narrow strait, where their ships cannot manoeuvre easily.

4 The Greeks suddenly turn and launch themselves at the Persians, who are thrown into confusion.

3 The Greek right wing, previously hidden from sight, attacks the Persian fleet in the flank, taking it by surprise.

1 The Corinthians and other Greeks hurriedly make sail in a seeming attempt to flee the Persian ships.

BATTLE OF GAUGAMELA

IN 331 BC, THE PERSIANS KNEW THEY HAD TO ARREST THE ADVANCE OF ALEXANDER THE GREAT.

Alexander's Macedonian/Greek army had scythed a path from the Balkans through Egypt and Palestine into Mesopotamia. Persian forces under emperor Darius III had already experienced a crushing defeat at Issus in 333 BC, and in 331 BC Alexander began making deeper incursions into Persian territory, heading for the river Tigris.

CAREFUL PREPARATION

Darius now gathered an army of enormous size in a final attempt to destroy the Macedonian advance. While Alexander commanded a force of around 47,000 Macedonian and Allied men, Darius manifested an army approaching a quarter of a million troops, including 40,000 elite Persian cavalry. The likeliest site of the subsequent battlefield is around Tel Gomel, east of Mosul in northern Iraq. Darius made the most careful of preparations. He established his troops in judicious positions in advance of Alexander's arrival and even flattened out the ground to allow his ➤➤

Alexander here meets with the family of Darius after the battle of Gaugamela. Darius was eventually stabbed to death by his own men, but his body was treated with the utmost respect by Alexander.

Above: A rather Europeanized image of Alexander and his horse, Bucephalos.
Right: That the Persians suffered disaster at Gaugamela is all the more remarkable when the near success of their encircling manoeuvre is viewed on this diagram.

cavalry greater ease of manoeuvre. Darius arranged his enormous army with a mixed infantry/cavalry force in the centre, cavalry on the flanks, and huge infantry resources forming a second line. The hope was to envelop the Macedonians using both speed and numbers. On 1 October 331 BC, the two sides drew into battle.

BREAKING LINES

The Persians opened the battle with a massive cavalry charge, but it soon became apparent that not everything was going according to the Persian plan. Alexander had built up his left flank purely as a holding force, resulting in the Persian line becoming skewed at an oblique angle across the Macedonian front. Persian cavalry did cut through Alexander's infantry, but Alexander had deliberately given ground to allow the breakthrough and he now simply closed the gap, leaving many Persian cavalry at the mercy of a rear reserve. Furthermore, a gap had opened up on the Persian left, through which Alexander poured his elite Companion Cavalry. Darius, who had placed himself in the centre, was now in personal danger of being surrounded, and he fled the battlefield. With the leader gone, the Persians collapsed and fled, leaving around 40,000 dead on the battlefield. ■

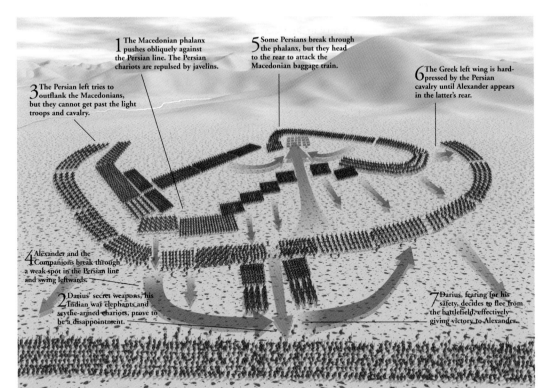

1 The Macedonian phalanx pushes obliquely against the Persian line. The Persian chariots are repulsed by javelins.

5 Some Persians break through the phalanx, but they head to the rear to attack the Macedonian baggage train.

3 The Persian left tries to outflank the Macedonians, but they cannot get past the light troops and cavalry.

6 The Greek left wing is hard-pressed by the Persian cavalry until Alexander appears in the latter's rear.

4 Alexander and the Companions break through a weak spot in the Persian line and swing leftwards.

2 Darius' secret weapons, his Indian war elephants and scythe-armed chariots, prove to be a disappointment.

7 Darius, fearing for his safety, decides to flee from the battlefield, effectively giving victory to Alexander.

ROMAN VICTORIES, ROMAN DEFEATS
300 BC – AD 450

The Roman Empire spawned one of the most professional armies in all of history. Its legionaries and cavalry expanded Rome's territories from the coasts of North Africa to the hinterlands of Britain, demonstrating a unique fighting cohesion and warrior spirit. The Roman skill at arms brought disaster to many armies, such as Hannibal's Carthaginians at Zama in 202 BC. However, Roman soldiers were not immune from major defeat – far from it. Overconfidence and geographical isolation periodically led the Romans to epic routs, including 50,000 Roman soldiers slaughtered at Cannae in 216 BC and the three Roman legions that died in the forests of the Teutoburger Wald in AD 9.

Left: 20,000 individuals were massacred over a period of three days in the Teutoburg forest in AD 9.

CANNAE

**IN THE SUMMER OF 216 BC, ROME WAS FIGHTING ON THE
BACK FOOT AGAINST WHAT WERE THE SEEMINGLY INVINCIBLE
CARTHAGINIAN FORCES OF HANNIBAL.**

In an attempt to turn the tide, a force of 80,000 soldiers was
assembled, commanded by L. Aemilius Paulus and C. Terrentius
Varro. Their army outnumbered the Carthaginians' by around
10,000 men, and all the Roman troops were of a high standard.
Hannibal himself had a mixed force, which included Gauls,
Spaniards and Numidians, as well as Carthaginians. As the two
forces met near the town of Cannae on the river Aufius, Varro
drew his legions into a classic Roman formation – three lines
of troops in the centre, with velites (light infantry armed with
throwing spears and a shield) occupying the first rank and the
heavy infantry the other two ranks; cavalry took both wings.

TACTICAL WITHDRAWAL

An initial Roman infantry charge seemed to work, and Hannibal's
centre gave way. Yet Hannibal had deployed his central ranks in a
crescent shape, with weaker Spanish and Gallic troops occupying ➤➤

Hannibal takes a vow to fight Rome until the bitter end, a vow he would fulfil in many ways. He ultimately ended his life as a fugitive from the Romans, and took poison un 183 BC to avoid capture.

Above: Hannibal's Numidian cavalry were renowned for travelling and fighting light, and were experts in using ground cover to launch ambushes. Right: The restrictive landscape at Cannae made the ordered Roman formations vulnerable to encirclement.

the front of the crescent, and toughened African troops located at the ends of the infantry lines. His cavalry, which was actually greater in number than that of the Romans, held flanking positions like the Romans.

MASSACRE

Although Hannibal's men appeared to be retreating, the collapse was actually a tactical one. The Roman infantry began to fall into a pincer trap, with the Carthaginian cavalry closing the jaws by driving away the cavalry on the infantry's right flank. Although the Romans initially could not see it, they were being enveloped in a semicircle of Carthaginian infantry. (At the beginning of the battle, Hannibal had pulled back large numbers of light infantry to the right of the flank, and these held their positions while the Romans advanced further down the centre to expose their flanks.) Soon the entire Roman infantry force was trapped in a Carthaginian encirclement, with Hannibal's cavalry controlling the Roman rear. A terrible slaughter ensued – 46,000 Romans were massacred and 22,000 became prisoners. Hannibal himself lost around 7000 men, and it was to prove the largest single defeat in Roman history. ∎

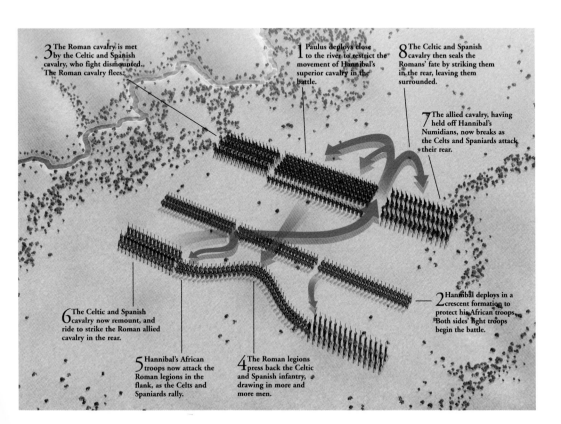

3 The Roman cavalry is met by the Celtic and Spanish cavalry, who fight dismounted. The Roman cavalry flees.

1 Paulus deploys close to the river to restrict the movement of Hannibal's superior cavalry in the battle.

8 The Celtic and Spanish cavalry then seals the Romans' fate by striking them in the rear, leaving them surrounded.

7 The allied cavalry, having held off Hannibal's Numidians, now breaks as the Celts and Spaniards attack their rear.

6 The Celtic and Spanish cavalry now remount, and ride to strike the Roman allied cavalry in the rear.

5 Hannibal's African troops now attack the Roman legions in the flank, as the Celts and Spaniards rally.

4 The Roman legions press back the Celtic and Spanish infantry, drawing in more and more men.

2 Hannibal deploys in a crescent formation to protect his African troops. Both sides' light troops begin the battle.

BATTLE OF ZAMA

THE BATTLE OF ZAMA WAS TO SEE THE COLLAPSE OF HANNIBAL'S EPIC MILITARY CAREER.

By 202 BC, the Second Punic War seemed to be drawing to a close. Between 210 and 206 BC the Carthaginians had lost Spain to the ascendant Roman general Scipio 'Africanus', who then forced Carthage to sue for peace by invading the kingdom in 204 BC. However, the negotiations broke down as Hannibal himself – along with 15,000 veterans – returned to Carthage from Italy. Once in Africa, Hannibal raised further troops (relying heavily on mercenaries) and set out to meet Scipio in battle.

CORRIDORS OF POWER

The battle of Zama (202 BC) saw each side possessing an army of around 35,000–40,000 men. Hannibal had three lines of infantry, his stalwart veterans in the rear line, with cavalry on the flanks and 50 war elephants in front. These were designed to smash open opposing lines at a charge, creating breaks for the infantry and cavalry to exploit. Scipio followed the same formation – infantry at the centre; cavalry in the flanks – and had arranged his soldiers ➤➤

KEY FACTS

Roman and Carthaginian armies (about 35,000 men each) meet at Regia Zama in 202 BC, led by Scipio 'Africanus' and Hannibal, respectively.

Carthaginian elephant charge defeated by Romans, who use corridors to channel the animals through the troops.

Hannibal's cavalry routed, and the Roman cavalry then turns on the Carthaginian rear as the Carthaginian infantry finally collapses under Roman assault.

The battle of Zama saw Hannibal's decisive defeat by the might of imperial Rome. Many ancient cavalry battles were decided by one side's cavalry finally gaining a flank advantage over its enemy, cutting off retreat or destroying formations.

*Above: A light cavalryman typical of
the Carthaginian army in the second
century BC. Hannibal applied several
different grades of cavalry to his battles,
ranging from light Numidian cavalry
through to heavy Spanish horse.*

in three lines, but he left corridors down through the infantry,
which were filled with skirmishing velites troops. The significance
of the corridors would become apparent once battle was joined.

FATAL CHARGE

Battle began when Hannibal launched his war elephants in a
charge against the Roman ranks. Some crashed into the main
Roman lines, but most of the beasts were naturally channelled
into the corridors. There the velites engaged them and their
drivers, driving them on down the corridors and out of the
battle. Now Hannibal faced a Roman charge. His front line of
mercenaries temporarily held the Roman infantry advance, but
Hannibal's cavalry was thrown back on both flanks by the
Romans and was driven from the field. Hannibal's first two
infantry lines then collapsed, and the Roman cavalry returned
from its pursuit to attack Hannibal's veterans at the rear.
Hannibal had been unable to outflank Scipio, who stretched his
infantry lines during battle to counter this very threat, and now
Hannibal found he was trapped. Carthaginian order disintegrated,
and defeat followed. Hannibal's military career was now in
precipitous decline, and no more victories were ahead of him.
He committed suicide in 182 or 183 BC. ■

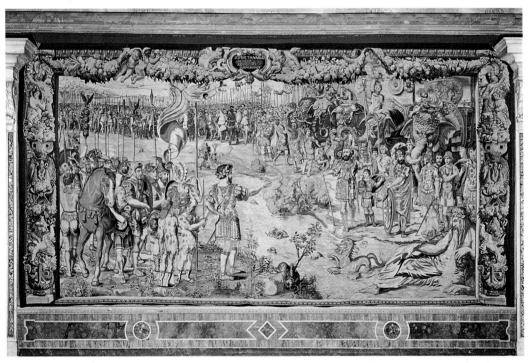

An exotic image of the Roman and Carthaginian armies facing one another at Zama. Visible are the Carthaginians' war elephants. Carthage used African Plains elephants, which were 'manned' by a crew of four.

BATTLE OF CARRHAE

THE CATASTROPHIC DEFEAT OF THE ROMAN LEGIONS AT THE BATTLE OF CARRHAE IN 53 BC STANDS AS A CLASSIC EXAMPLE OF MILITARY HUBRIS.

The Roman senator Marcus Crassus was eager to match the military triumphs of his peers Caesar and Pompey. He decided on Mesopotamia as his battleground, and the Parthians as his enemy. The Parthians at this time had a professional military, which utilized heavily armoured horsemen (known as 'cataphracts') alongside highly nimble horse archers to outmanoeuvre and abrade enemy ranks. Crassus totally underestimated the level of threat, and rejected excellent strategic advice from the king of Armenia, who recommended using high ground to break up Parthian cavalry charges.

ATTACK AND RETREAT

In 53 BC, Crassus marched into Mesopotamia with a force of 44,000 men, choosing a scorching desert route that made both forage and water scarce (his ultimate objective was Seleucia on the Tigris). Here some 11,000 Parthian horsemen began to make ➤➤

KEY FACTS

53 BC – defeat of 44,000 Roman troops by around 11,000 Parthian cavalry.

Parthians outmanoeuvred Romans with mounted archers and armoured cavalry applying hit-and-run tactics.

The Romans, commanded by Crassus, did not field enough cavalry to counter the Parthian threat.

The Parthians applied a classic rule of military tactics – do not fight on your enemy's terms – to inflict a massive defeat upon Roman forces. Crassus' failure was to underestimate his enemy and ignore experienced tactical advice.

Above: The classic Roman helmet as worn by a legionary soldier, featuring a horsehair plume – these were usually natural in colour.

Right: The diagram clearly shows the Parthian breaking of the Roman square.

swarming 'hit and run' attacks on the Roman columns, each attack light in isolation, but gradually inflicting a significant toll on men and morale. Crassus formed his men into defensive squares, but this achieved little more than making a condensed target for the enemy archers. The Parthian commander Surenas had also deployed a force of 1000 camels to resupply the archers with arrows on the battlefield itself.

FEIGNED RETREAT

Crassus' next tactical gambit was to launch his own cavalry and archers against the enemy horsemen. The Roman cavalry – headed by Crassus' son, Publius – seemed to be making headway, but fell for a classic Parthian tactic, the feigned retreat. Publius' force was isolated and destroyed to a man, with Publius' head cut off and stuck on a lance for the benefit of the Romans.

Now Crassus called a withdrawal, but the Romans' fate was sealed. Although about 10,000 Romans managed to escape, the rest were either killed or captured on the long retreat. Crassus himself, having tried to negotiate a surrender, was captured and beheaded. His head was put on show in the Parthian court, as were the standards of the decimated Legions. ■

2 The Romans launch local counterattacks, but the Parthians evade them easily, showering the Romans with arrows.

1 The Parthians charge at the Roman square in a column to disguise their numbers, but break off and surround it instead.

4 The 'fleeing' Parthians draw Publius away from the main Roman body, before wheeling about and charging him.

5 Publius' detachment is cut down by Parthian arrows and cataphract charges. To avoid capture, Publius commits suicide.

3 Publius is sent with a detachment against some of the Parthians, who apparently flee. Publius gives chase.

6 The Roman square suffers further cataphract charges and showers of arrows. They finally escape after dark.

BATTLE OF ACTIUM

IN 31 BC, ROME WAS STRICKEN BY ONE OF ITS PERENNIAL POLITICAL POWER STRUGGLES.

Following the murder of Julius Caesar in 44 BC, the Roman empire had been split between Octavian (later Augustus), who controlled Italy and the western Mediterranean, and Marc Anthony, who took the Near East and Greece, and also married Queen Cleopatra VII of Egypt. The union with Cleopatra followed Anthony's rejection of marriage to Octavian's sister, and the two men were drawn into war for the leadership of the Roman empire.

FORCES DEPLETED

The decisive battle took place near the entrance to the Ambracian Gulf, on the coast of western Greece. On 2 September 31 BC, Anthony led a fleet of around 230 ships into disaster. Anthony's fate turned against him even before the battle was joined. He had anchored his ships in the swamplands of Cape Actium, where malaria took away many of his oarsmen. There had also been large numbers of desertions owing to the unpopularity ➤➤

KEY FACTS

Battle takes place on 2 September 31 BC, with 230 ships under Marc Anthony facing the 400 smaller ships of Octavian.

Anthony's fleet attempts to punch through Octavian's flank, but fails to make headway, and Octavian's fleet counterattacks.

Cleopatra and Anthony flee the battle, leaving 170 vessels to be destroyed.

Imperial troops watch the complete destruction of the war fleet of Anthony and Cleopatra. Illness, desertion, loss of sleep and political problems were as much the causes of Anthony's disaster as enemy action.

of his Egyptian marriage alliance, so Anthony's force was much depleted when it faced Octavian's 400 vessels ranked across the mouth of the Gulf of Ambracia, commanded by admiral Agrippa. Eventually, Anthony sailed his fleet out to battle. He hoped to use his heavy warships to make ramming attacks against the enemy flanks; however, Agrippa kept his ships skilfully out of range, in order to exhaust the reduced crews of the opposing vessels.

PIECEMEAL DESTRUCTION

When Agrippa finally committed to fight, the forces closed in blistering exchanges of catapult, arrow and sling fire, while boarding parties fought hand-to-hand on enemy decks. It was clear that Anthony was losing the battle, and Cleopatra's supporting force of 60 vessels fled south with its queen. Anthony soon joined her, and left his mariners to their fate. Without any effective leadership whatsoever, Anthony's fleet was thrown into complete disarray. One by one the ships were destroyed, Agrippa's troops using fire weapons to ignite on-board blazes. Only 60 of Anthony's warships escaped the destruction. While Octavian went on to be the greatest of Rome's emperors, Marc Anthony would commit suicide in 30 BC. ■

Above: The ill-fated couple Anthony and Cleopatra.

Right: The map of the battle shows how the Egyptian naval forces were trapped across the Gulf of Ambracia.

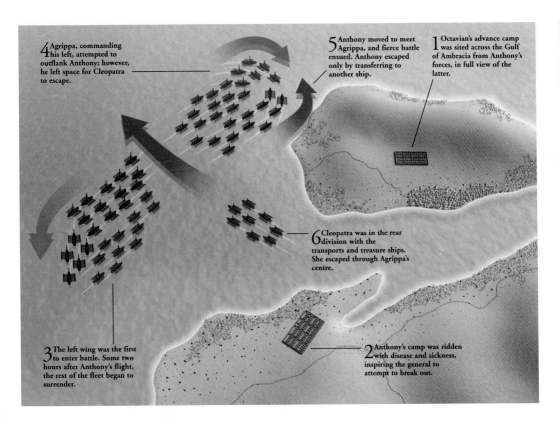

4 Agrippa, commanding his left, attempted to outflank Anthony; however, he left space for Cleopatra to escape.

5 Anthony moved to meet Agrippa, and fierce battle ensued. Anthony escaped only by transferring to another ship.

1 Octavian's advance camp was sited across the Gulf of Ambracia from Anthony's forces, in full view of the latter.

6 Cleopatra was in the rear division with the transports and treasure ships. She escaped through Agrippa's centre.

3 The left wing was the first to enter battle. Some two hours after Anthony's flight, the rest of the fleet began to surrender.

2 Anthony's camp was ridden with disease and sickness, inspiring the general to attempt to break out.

TEUTOBURGER WALD

AT THE BEGINNING OF THE FIRST MILLENNIUM AD, THE ROMAN EMPIRE WAS PARTICULARLY TROUBLED IN ITS NORTHERN EUROPEAN TERRITORIES.

In AD 6, Publius Quinctilius Varus was appointed governor to Germania, and one of his first responsibilities was to continue the work of Tiberias (the previous governor) in subduing and consolidating the region. In AD 9, Varus, along with some Germanic allies, was operating in frontier territories with a large force consisting of three Legions (numbered XVII, XVIII and XIX), six cohorts and three squadrons of cavalry – a total of 15,000 troops. Alongside them were the soldiers of the Cherusci tribe, led by chief Arminius.

GUERILLA WARFARE

Arminius had offered the services of his men in suppressing various rebellions in the region, although he actually had other plans. Varus had done a reasonably good job of alienating most of the Germanic tribes through tax arrangements and imperial philosophy, and Arminius was not the ally he pretended to be. ➤➤

KEY FACTS

- **AD 9** – Roman forces under Varus betrayed by supposed Germanic ally Arminius, and are ambushed in the Teutoburg forest.
- **Three Roman** Legions, assorted other units and camp followers murdered over three days in the Teutoburg forest.
- **Varus commits** suicide, one of 20,000 Roman deaths.

The Roman leader Publius Quinctilius Varus prepares to commit suicide as his legions are slaughtered around him in the Teutoburg forest. Varus imposed harsh financial arrangements on colonized peoples which lost him local support.

A Roman legionary, seen here carrying a standard. A special campaign was launched to recover the standards lost in the Teutoburg forest.

In fact, Varus received warning of a potential Cherusci uprising, but chose to ignore the concerns.

INTO THE TRAP

Varus' retreat back towards winter quarters took him through the forbidding Teutoburger Wald, a densely forested region that fractured the Roman formations. Near modern-day Detmold, Arminius and his troops disappeared, and from this point on the unfortunate Romans were subjected to constant attacks by German tribes, who used guerrilla methods to which the Romans had no adequate response. The Romans could not mount effective counter-strikes, and the presence of heavy baggage and civilian camp followers further hampered mobility. Over the course of three days, the entire Roman column, totalling around 20,000 individuals, was massacred in the forests. Varus himself committed suicide with his sword; the Germans cut off his head and sent it to Augustus. For the Romans, it was an utter catastrophe, and they were never able to exert full control over the German frontier. ■

The disaster in the Teutoburger Wald became a favourite of artists for centuries afterwards, despite the fact that for almost 2000 years no one could pinpoint the exact site of the battle.

BATTLE OF ADRIANOPLE

IN THE LATE FOURTH CENTURY AD, THE ROMAN EMPIRE WAS GOVERNED IN TWO PARTS, A WESTERN EMPIRE UNDER GRATIAN AND AN EASTERN EMPIRE UNDER GRATIAN'S UNCLE VALENS.

The origins of the battle of Adrianople lay in the displacement of the Visigothic people north of the Black Sea by invading Huns, and certain tribes were permitted to cross into imperial territory to settle along the Danube. However, harsh Roman rule caused the Danubian Visigoths to rebel, and Ostrogothic peoples of the Greuthungi tribe also crossed the Danube to join them in this rebellion. It was against these rampaging Goths that Valens and Gratian marshalled their forces.

PREMATURE ENGAGEMENT

Although Valens was engaged in war with Persia at that time, he redeployed to face the threat from the Goths. Gratian's army was also engaged, but on 9 August 378 he fought a unilateral action with 40,000 soliders, at a site around 13km (8 miles) north of Adrianople (just west of Istanbul). He had discovered the Goths in a classic circular camp (known as a *laager*), with wagons acting ➤➤

KEY FACTS

- **9 August** AD 378 – Valens attacks Gothic encampment north of Adrianople with about 40,000 troops.
- **The Gothic** encampment, which is circular in formation, resists Roman attempts to break in.
- **The Gothic** cavalry returns from a foraging trip and destroys the Roman force, killing Valens and about 30,000 soldiers.

Foreign policy was a fickle and turbulent affair in fourth century Europe. Here the Emperor Valens is seen making a treaty with the leaders of the Visigoths, only two years before the massacre at Adrianople.

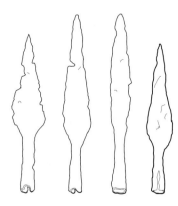

Outlines of time-battered spear heads from the time of Adrianople. The protection provided by the Gothic laager *would have rendered the Roman spear offensive indecisive, especially as the circular formation of the* laager *would have broken the Roman linear phalanx.*

as an outer wall. This structure made it difficult for the Romans to assault in their usual linear formations, but the Gothic cavalry was momentarily absent, so Valens decided to waste no time. He first attacked with his cavalry, attempting to batter his way into the *laager*. The Gothics replied tenaciously, firing arrows and hurling spears from behind the wagons, and the Romans were unable to split the defence.

OUTCLASSED AND OVERWHELMED

Suddenly the Gothic heavy cavalry reappeared. It was a moment of crisis for the Romans. Their own light cavalry was completely outclassed by the heavy Gothic horse, and the Roman mounts were driven from the battle, taking appalling casualties. The Gothic cavalry now began to hew down the Roman infantry, who lost their usual capacity to extricate themselves from trouble. A massacre ensued; the total number of Roman casualties is unknown, but may number as much as 30,000 men. Valens was included among the dead, and he became one of the thousands of anonymous corpses left to rot on the battlefield. ■

A German woodcut depicts refugees migrating westwards to avoid an approaching invasion of the Huns. The Huns were responsible for the displacement of both Ostrogothic and Visigothic peoples, and were renowed for their martial skills, but were finally brought under control by a coalition of European tribes in the mid fifth century.

THE DARK AGES
450 – 1100

The early centuries of the first millennium were a time of great social and political turbulence in Europe and Asia. Goths, Huns, Byzantines, Franks, Muslims and many other peoples vied for territorial supremacy in various corners of the world, resulting in a terrible frequency of war and destructive conquest. The military disasters of this world were hacked out with the awful tools of war specific to the period, such as the battle-axe, mace, short sword and lance. In addition, the battles could be fought with a conspicuous lack of mercy, with whole armies, even entire cities, being put to the sword during and after the main action.

Left: Some 50,000 – 90,000 people were put to the sword at the siege and fall of Jerusalem in 1099.

BATTLE OF VOUILLÉ

AT THE BEGINNING OF THE SIXTH CENTURY, THE EMPIRE OF
THE VISIGOTHS HAD REACHED ITS PEAK IN GAUL. WITH ITS
CAPITAL IN TOULOUSE, IT INCLUDED ALMOST ALL OF THE
IBERIAN PENINSULA AND AQUITAINE, AS WELL AS CONQUESTS
UP THE LOIRE VALLEY.

At this time, the leader of the Visigoths was Alaric II, who
generally attempted moderate politics, reducing the persecution
of Catholic believers that had been followed by his predecessors.

A MILITARY ROUT

Alaric practised Arianism, a fourth-century form of Christianity,
which denied the divinity of Christ. It was this very Arianism that
would bring Alaric into war with the Franks under their ruler,
Clovis. Clovis, a bloody and single-minded warrior king, was
looking for a pretext to extend the Frankish kingdom into the
Visigothic territories of southern Gaul. The Franks were Catholic,
so with Alaric's conversion to Arianism, Clovis had found the
perfect excuse to carry out his expansion plans. Accordingly, the
two armies met in battle near Poitiers, at Vouillé – a site also ➤➤

KEY FACTS

The Visigoths under Alaric II
face the Franks of Clovis at
the battle of Vouillé, near
Poitiers, in 507.

The Visigoths are routed,
and Alaric is personally slain
by Clovis.

The Visigoths lose control
of almost all their territories
in Gaul.

The Visigoths were rightly considered a ferocious battlefield enemy. The battle-axe was a principal weapon, the infantry generally using a two-handed weapon, while the cavalry favoured a single-handed weapon ideal for splitting open enemy armour plate.

Heavily stylized images of the Frankish ruler Clovis (left), stood alongside his queen, Clotilde.

known as Campus Vogladensis – at the northern edges of the Visigothic kingdom in 507.

GOTHIC DISASTER

The battle of Vouillé looked set to be a disaster for the Visigoths from the start. The numbers of soldiers involved on both sides are unclear; however, as well as his own army, Clovis had allied himself with Anastasius I of the Byzantine empire, who drew in forces from eastern Gaul against Alaric. When the opposing sides finally clashed, the Visigoths found themselves outclassed by the ferocity of the Frankish warriors, who hewed down hundreds of Goths with their heavy battle-axes and swords. Alaric himself was not to escape this fate. Seeing the rout of his army, Alaric fled the field, with Clovis himself in pursuit. Clovis overtook Alaric, and personally cut him down, although Clovis narrowly escaped death himself when attacked by two Gothic lancers (Gregory of Tours tells us he was saved by his coat of mail and a very fast horse). The battle of Vouillé resulted in a major territorial loss for the Visigoths, as southern France passed into the hands of the Franks and the Visigoths were pushed down into the Iberian peninsula. ■

King Clovis I stands by his throne. Clovis lived from 465 to 511, and was the Franks' first Christian ruler.

BATTLE OF DARA

IN THE EARLY YEARS OF THE SIXTH CENTURY, THE BYZANTINES WERE EAGER TO GUARD THEIR EMERGING EMPIRE AGAINST PERSIAN INCURSIONS FROM THE EAST.

The defensive measures included the construction of a fort ('Dara') on the Mesopotamian frontier in what is today Syria. The fortress dominated important trade roads in the region, and created intense political tension between the Byzantines and the Persians. In 527, the Byzantine emperor Justinian I began a war with the Sassanids (a Persian dynasty that reigned in Persia between 224 and 651). In 530, after some Byzantine defeats, the Persian king Kavadh I directed a force of 40,000 men against the Dara fortress, commanded by the general Firouz.

HIDDEN FORCES

The strong Persian force marched to Dara probably expecting a prolonged siege action, and they initially encamped at Ammodius, about 5km (3 miles) from the Byzantine strongpoint. They then marched out to the fortress, where they found that Belisarius, the Byzantine general, had brought his troops out to attack, forming ➤➤

KEY FACTS

- **c.506** – the Byzantines construct a fortress outpost (Dara) on the frontier with Persia.
- **530** – Kavadh I of Persia attacks the fortress with a total force of 50,000 men against the 25,000 troops under Belisarius.
- **The Persian army** is split by a Byzantine cavalry ambush, and is defeated with more than 5000 dead.

Belisarius is given a triumphal reception in Rome following a military victory. Belisarius began his military career as a bodyguard to the emperor Justinian, but was given command positions at the age of only 25.

Another image of the great military leader Belisarius, following his political downfall in later life. He actually lived out his later years in peace, in some recognition of his state service.

them up in battle lines. The Persians – who outnumbered the Byzantines by two-to-one – quickly launched into the attack, making a serious impression on the Heruli on the Byzantine right flank, but eventually being forced back. There followed a curious break in action when a Persian warrior threw out a challenge for single combat, and was subsequently killed by a Heruli soldier called Andreas, who also dispatched a further challenger. Both sides then withdrew, the Persians heading back to Ammodius.

PERSIAN CATASTROPHE

The next day saw battle rejoined, the Persians buttressed by 10,000 additional troops from Nisibis. After an indecisive arrow battle, the Persians charged again and began to push back the Byzantine centre. Unknown to them, however, Belisarius had positioned a hidden cavalry behind a hill to the left of Dara. He now flung them against the stretched Persian flank, and with coordinated attacks from Hun infantry managed to cleave the Persian army in two. At the same time, the Byzantine cavalry overcame their mounted opponents, and the Persian army collapsed. More than 5000 Persians died on the battlefield. Only in 573 did the Persians finally take Dara. ∎

The once mighty Belisarius fell foul of politics in 562 AD, when the emperor Justinian accused him of conspiracy and imprisoned him for several months. Legend asserts that he was blinded and forced to beg, but this is untrue.

BATTLE OF TOURS

THE BATTLE OF TOURS IN 733 OR 734 (ALSO KNOWN TO HISTORY AS THE BATTLE OF POITIERS) WAS A DECISIVE ENGAGEMENT IN THE POLITICAL HISTORY OF WESTERN EUROPE.

By the beginning of the eighth century, militaristic Islam had taken over most of the Middle East, Central Asia and North Africa, and in 711 attacked western Europe, first conquering Spain. In 732, however, the Frankish empire was ascendant in much of Europe, particularly Gaul, and the Muslim governor of Spain, Abd ar-Rahman, decided to settle the issue of regional power. Crossing the Pyrenees with an army that may have numbered upwards of 400,000 men (though more conservative estimates place the figure as low as 60,000), he marched towards the Loire valley.

STERN RESISTANCE
Resisting Abd ar-Rahman was the Frankish army under Charles Martel. Martel was commanding a purely infantry force, whereas the Muslims had a high percentage of elite armoured Saracen cavalry, which had served them well in previous conquests. The forces met on the edge of a forested area near the city of Tours, ➤➤

➤➤

KEY FACTS

733 or 734 – a huge Muslim army commanded by Abd ar-Rahman invades France from Spain. It joins battle with the Franks of Charles Martel around Tours.

Arab cavalry is unable to break open the Frankish infantry formations.

Abd ar-Rahman is killed and Muslim order collapses after their treasure stores are threatened; they make an overnight retreat.

A vivid image of the battle of Tours. A typical Frankish foot soldier might be armed with a shield and lance, and short sword, and a bow with around a dozen arrows, the bow also having a spare string.

A Frankish infantryman seen here with shield and a fearsome-looking mace. Frankish foot soldiers also used a heavy shield-splitting axe known as a Francisca, which could be thrown as well as gripped.

and the Muslims were already facing certain disadvantages. Their clothes were unsuited to the intense seasonal cold, and the broken terrain was not ideal for their cavalry. Nevertheless, they charged, the cavalry slashing down upon the Frankish infantry. However, Martel had deployed his troops in dense, heavily armed phalanx formations, and his troops stood firm under even the most hacking attacks (with the river Loire to their backs, they could not have retreated anyway).

MUSLIM INFIGHTING

On several occasions, it looked as though the French might buckle, but they endured and also managed an attack against the Muslim treasure stores (the Muslims had taken huge bounty from operations in Bordeaux). Responding to this financial crisis, the Muslim forces broke ranks and order disintegrated. Furthermore, Abd ar-Rahman was killed by an enemy spear. The Muslim forces now retreated back to their camp, and internal fighting occurred against the Muslim troops as they tried to restore their property. Sources are confused over whether the battle lasted for one or several days, but after their defeat the Muslims retreated back over the Pyrenees. The collapse was a bitter blow for Muslim ambitions in western Europe, and finally showed the limits of their cavalry superiority. ■

Muslim soldiers engage with their European enemies. Their swords were probably much straighter than this depiction presents.

JERUSALEM

THE SIEGE AND FALL OF JERUSALEM IN 1099 WAS A MILITARY DISASTER (FOR THE DEFENDERS), AND TURNED INTO A GREAT HUMAN TRAGEDY.

In 1098, after a 48-day siege, Jerusalem fell under Muslim rule, and so became a prime objective of the Christian knights and infantry of the First Crusade (1095–100), who had advanced from the Balkans into the Holy Land by 1097. Predicting the Crusaders' arrival, the Muslim garrison of Jerusalem, led by the capable commander Iftikhar al-Dawla, repaired damage to the outer walls, and built up the earthwork and ditch defences ringing the city. They also prepared for a siege, stockpiling food and water, cutting down local trees to deny the crusaders use of timber, and poisoning wells outside the city to reduce the enemy's water supply. Al-Dalwa also expelled many of the city's Christians.

A RUTHLESS VICTORY

Initially, al-Dawla's measures seemed to pay off. The crusaders reached Jerusalem on 7 June 1099 and attacked it on 13 June, with no success. Hence they began a siege action. Around 1500 knights ➤➤

KEY FACTS

1098 – Jerusalem is occupied by Muslim forces after a 48-day siege.

13 June 1099 – Christian forces of the First Crusade put Jerusalem under siege.

15 July – Jerusalem falls to the Crusaders, who massacre the city's entire population, with up to 90,000 people being killed.

The Muslim defenders of Jerusalem greet the Crusader arrivals with insults and missiles.

A Crusader foot soldier. He wears a hauberk (a mail shirt) with a typical conical helmet and a kite-shaped shield (many shields had more of a triangular configuration).

and 5000 infantry ringed Jerusalem, but their numbers were quickly reduced by lack of water and food, and spreading disease. However, a fleet of Christian ships arrived at Jaffa on 17 June, and the ships' timbers were used to make three siege towers, completed during the first week of July. On 13 July, the Crusaders began to advance the towers towards the walls of Jerusalem. Initial efforts failed, but one tower managed to site itself next to the northeastern gate on 15 July, and the Crusaders began flooding into the city.

SLAUGHTER OF THE INNOCENTS

What happened next is one of the most appalling episodes in Christian history. The Crusaders systematically killed almost every man, woman and child in the city. Brutalized by long months of war and hardship, the soldiers massacred almost all they came upon, including Christians, and slaughtered a vast crowd of refugees in the al-Aqsa mosque. One contemporary account observed that 'the slaughter was so great that our men waded in blood up to their ankles'. Ironically, only al-Dawla and his bodyguard survived, after they surrendered when trapped by enemy soldiers. It has been estimated that some 50,000–90,000 people were put to the sword in Jerusalem. In Christian Europe, bells were rung to celebrate the 'victory'. ■

The Crusades were seen as the archetypal 'holy wars', and the soldiery would be accompanied by a large numbers of priests and ministers, most of whom saw nothing theologically wrong in the massacre of Jerusalem's population.

MEDIEVAL MELEES
1100 – 1500

The medieval period saw a steady transformation in warfare, particularly from the fourteenth century with the introduction of gunpowder weaponry onto the battlefield. Medieval cannon and small arms would initially have a limited effect upon the outcome of a fight, but they had important implications for the future. The new firepower not only threatened the walls of cities and fortifications, but also enabled the lowliest peasant soldier, with the minimum of training, to take the advantage over an aristocratic knight with centuries of military tradition behind him. However, as Agincourt would prove, older weaponry was still capable of inflicting disaster upon an opposing force.

Left: The fighting at Bosworth field in 1485 ended with Richard III being dragged down from his horse and impaled on spikes.

HATTIN

THE BATTLE OF HATTIN WAS A CRUSHING DEFEAT FOR THE CRUSADERS OF THE LATE TWELFTH CENTURY.

Muslim forces under Saladin had besieged the town of Tiberias on the western shores of the Sea of Galilee, threatening Jerusalem. About 32km (20 miles) away at Sephoria, however, was a large Crusader army under King Guy of Jerusalem, which contained up to 20,000 infantry and more than 1200 cavalry. The Crusaders' strategic decision-making was plagued by argument and personal rivalries. One of the senior leaders, Raymond III of Tripoli, argued against attacking Saladin around Tiberias, as Muslim forces were at their best on open ground. Instead, he recommended a defensive action at Sephoria, but he was overridden by King Guy. On 3 July, the Crusaders set out for Tiberias, ranked up in three large divisions.

WEAKENED BY THIRST

By early morning, the Crusader army was under harassing attack from Muslim mounted archers, who concentrated particularly on Guy's rearguard. The attacks not only caused many casualties, ➤➤

KEY FACTS

- **3 July 1187** – Crusader army under King Guy of Jerusalem moves against Muslim forces at Tiberias, but comes under attack soon into the advance.
- **Crusader army** critically weakened prior to main battles by lack of water and Muslim hit-and-run attacks.
- **Only 3000** Crusaders escape the Muslims out of an initial force of around 25,000.

A moment of subjugation – an English soldier falls at the feet of the Muslim leader Saladin.

but also kept forcing the Christian army to stop. Soon the Crusaders were becoming desperate for water, a situation which was exacerbated when they had to make night camp in an arid plain near Maskana.

RUNNING DRY

The next day, the deteriorating Crusader force made ready for battle near the Horns of Hattin, an extinct volcano which held the promise of spring water. However, many of the Crusader infantry had now deserted into the Horns of Hattin itself, and the Crusader cavalry made three fruitless, bloody charges against the massed infantry and cavalry of the Muslims that were now encircling Guy's force. Eventually, even the surviving cavalry fled to the Horns of Hattin to seek refuge.

The Crusader army eventually collapsed through lack of water and appalling casualties. Final death tolls are unknown, as the Muslims took many prisoners, but it is understood that only around 3000 Crusaders eventually made it to safety. It was the start of a series of catastrophic defeats for the Crusading nations, culminating in the fall of Jerusalem on 2 October. ■

The two pikemen are protected by the fire of the crossbowmen behind them. The most powerful crossbows could puncture armour and kill the wearer at more than 150m (492ft).

Crusaders captured by the Muslims faced either execution or, if they were fortunate, a life of total slavery.

STIRLING BRIDGE

THE ENGLISH DISASTER AT STIRLING BRIDGE ON 11 SEPTEMBER 1297 WAS THE RESULT OF YET ANOTHER FAILED ATTEMPT TO CRUSH THE REBELLIOUS SCOTS OF WILLIAM WALLACE.

The expedition was led by John de Warrenne, Earl of Surrey, who had been appointed as governor of Scotland, and he was accompanied by the corpulent Hugh de Cressingham as Scotland's new treasurer.

TACTICAL MISTAKE

The English soon reached a major natural obstacle, the river Forth, which ran just beneath the town of Stirling. Unbeknown to Warrenne, however, the Scottish rebels were already in position in wooded high ground near Cambuskenneth Abbey, overlooking the river. Led by Wallace and Sir Andrew Murray, the rebels were in many ways a ragtag army, most of low social rank and many armed with home-made weaponry, but they had the advantage of terrain over the English, who were now debating the best way of crossing the river. The most obvious crossing point was the narrow wooden Stirling Bridge, an easy route instantly favoured by the ➤➤

KEY FACTS

- **11 September 1297** – Scottish troops under William Wallace ambush an English force
- **Massive defeat** for the English forces of John de Warrenne, with around 5500 English troops killed.
- **English force** makes critical tactical error, choosing to cross the river Forth over the narrow Stirling Bridge.

The English decision to cross Stirling Bridge precipitated a great disaster. The English soldiers had made two earlier attempts to cross the bridge, but on both occasions had been recalled.

The tactical skill and warrior spirit of the Scottish soldier shocked the English, who had not lost a major battle to the Scots since the Dark Ages.

militarily inexperienced Warrenne. However, veteran soldiers such as Sir Ralph Lundy pointed out that the bridge could only be crossed two abreast, and a safer ford for a cavalry backup was to be found around a mile away.

INTO THE TRAP

Lundy's advice was ignored, and the English began crossing Stirling Bridge, Sir Marmaduke Twenge and Hugh de Cressingham forming the lead. A trap was opening up. The ground over the other side of the river was boggy, and generally unsuitable for cavalry movement. Furthermore, the curve in the river prevented the English from making a proper battle formation. Wallace waited until around half the English army had crossed, then attacked. It was an utter slaughter. The English were not able to organize to fight coherently, and they could not be reinforced as the other half of the army was stuck across the other side of the river. The Scots hewed down the English horses, then killed the mounted soldiers once they had fallen into the boggy ground. In less than an hour, the English force was routed. Hugh de Cressingham himself was killed. In a grim testimony to the English disaster, Cressingham's body was skinned and the skin cut up for souvenirs. ∎

The trial of William Wallace, conducted in Westminster Hall, London. Sentenced to death for treason, Wallace was hung until near death, then disembowelled and beheaded. Parts of his body were sent for public display across England and Scotland.

BANNOCKBURN

IN 1314, THE LONG-RUNNING WAR BETWEEN THE ENGLISH AND THE SCOTS CULMINATED IN THE FORCES OF ROBERT THE BRUCE BESIEGING STIRLING CASTLE.

The English king Edward II raised a relief force of 2500 cavalry and 14,000 infantry/men-at-arms and took it north of the border to face Robert's 10,000 infantry and 300 light horse.

CAUGHT IN TRAPS

The English would have been looking back to their defeat of the Scots at Falkirk in 1298, when the forces of Edward I applied archers and cavalry to break up the Scottish shiltrons (densely packed formations of infantry formed into a spear shape). On 23 June, Edward's forces approached Stirling from the south over a boggy area of ground known as the 'Carse'. Across this ran the Bannockburn, a stream roughly 5km (3 miles) long, and an obstacle which would have to be forded by the English troops. As they closed on the burn, English soldiers discovered that the Scots had dug man traps around the stream and surrounding fields, consisting of narrow holes about 60cm (24in) deep with sharpened stakes at the bottom. Numerous men and horses were injured by the pits, but the English ploughed on. The first actual clash of arms occurred when the vaunted English warrior Henry de Bohun faced Robert the ➤

KEY FACTS

1314 – An English force under Edward II advances into Scotland to raise the siege of Stirling Castle.

23 June – The two sides clash around Bannockburn. The English are beaten off and make camp for the night.

24 June – The Scots attack the Engish camp at first light, overwhelming the defenders. Edward II flees.

Robert the Bruce achieved his crowning military glory at Bannockburn. The Scottish forces utilized ambush, terrain and guerrilla-style attacks to undermine the typical English superiority in numbers.

➤➤

Bruce himself in a one-to-one action. Much to the dismay of his subordinates, the English knight was quickly dispatched by Bruce with a battle-axe. Furthermore, a unit of 300 English cavalry under Sir Robert Clifford was unable to penetrate and defeat a defensive block of 300 pike-bearing Scots arranged in schiltrons. The burn crossing was called off, and the English made camp for the night, the straggling army having arrived piecemeal during the day.

FIRST-LIGHT ATTACK

To take advantage of the English disorder, Robert launched a major attack at first light the next day (24 June). Exploding out of the surrounding woods at around 3 a.m., the Scots raced into the British camp, preventing the sleepy English cavalry and archers from making formation. The cavalry found itself having to fight on foot, and was pushed back by the schiltrons into the marshy ground. Wading into the mud, many were then killed by the more nimble Scots. Facing a rout, the English began to panic, the only moment of light being when a group of archers began to take a toll on the Scots. However, these were dispatched by about 350 Scottish cavalry, and defeat was now inevitable. Edward II fled the battlefield, and the English force totally collapsed. It had been a dreadful catastrophe for the English. ■

Right: The English were comprehensively routed at Bannockburn, victims of Robert the Bruce's tactical initiative and the boggy terrain which was unsuited to the English heavy cavalry.

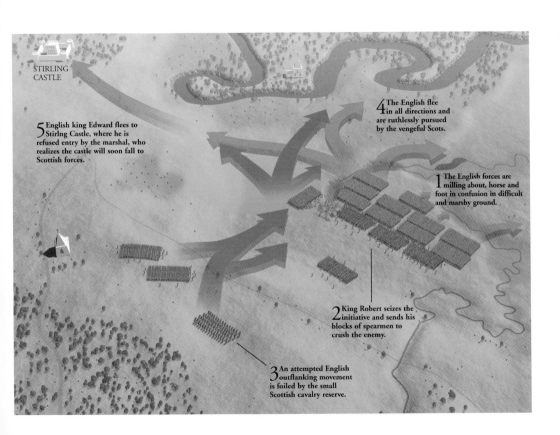

STIRLING
CASTLE

5 English king Edward flees to Stirlng Castle, where he is refused entry by the marshal, who realizes the castle will soon fall to Scottish forces.

4 The English flee in all directions and are ruthlessly pursued by the vengeful Scots.

1 The English forces are milling about, horse and foot in confusion in difficult and marshy ground.

2 King Robert seizes the initiative and sends his blocks of spearmen to crush the enemy.

3 An attempted English outflanking movement is foiled by the small Scottish cavalry reserve.

CRÉCY

THE BATTLE OF CRÉCY WAS A CRITICAL FRENCH DISASTER IN THE HUNDRED YEARS WAR (1337–1453).

Moreover, it was a disaster caused, in the main, not by faulty French tactics, but by a shift in battlefield technologies.

A REDUNDANT CAVALRY

On 12 July 1346, an English force of around 15,000 troops commanded by Edward III had landed in Normandy, and commenced a month of raiding, which included an attack on Paris in mid-August. By this time, Philip VI's French army was in hot pursuit, with a total strength of around 30,000 troops. The French tactical mind-set was centred on the use of cavalry, and Philip was naturally assured that his cavalry could overwhelm Edward's much smaller cavalry contingent.

On 26 August, the French army finally closed with the English on an area of sloping land between Crécy and Wadicourt. Crucially, Edward had chosen and prepared the site in advance, placing his several thousand longbowmen on the crest of the hill, while laying a system of ditches and traps (including hundreds of ➤➤

KEY FACTS

- **26 August 1346** – battle of Crécy fought between English invading force of Edward III and French army of Philip VI.
- **French force** attempts a traditional cavalry battle; English army uses archery, infantry and obstacles to break up and slaughter the French charge.
- **French army** suffers around 30 per cent casualties, and is forced to withdraw.

The French cavalry at Crécy was not only the victim of archery, but also of crude defensive ditchwork which broke horses' legs.

metal caltrops) in front of his infantry to bring down the French horses. Philip, meanwhile, had arranged his army into two main ranks – with about 6000 Genoese crossbowmen to the front, and the mass of cavalry behind.

FIREPOWER

The battle began at about 5 p.m. The Genoese troops advanced, firing salvos of bolts on the English. The English archers, however, replied with a devastating rain of arrows, which outranged and outnumbered the enemy bolts: the archers could fire up to 12 arrows a minute; the crossbowmen only 3–5 bolts a minute. French troops were being slaughtered where they stood, and with the Genoese in retreat Philip ordered a cavalry charge. Against expectations, the English did not meet cavalry with cavalry, but remained on foot. The French charge was broken up by the obstacles and incline of the hill, and the French knights were shot from their horses by close-range arrow fire. By nightfall, a wounded Philip accepted French defeat and withdrew his forces. Philip's army had suffered around 12,000 casualties (some accounts suggest up to 30,000); the English fewer than 500. The defeat brought about crisis in the French court, and contributed to widespread social and political unrest. ■

The battle of Crécy was as much about a clash of firepower as about close-quarters combat. While the French crossbows had a better penetrative power at shorter ranges, the English longbows had higher rates of fire, and these proved decisive.

NICOPOLIS

BY THE LATE FOURTEENTH CENTURY, THE FORCES OF THE SEEMINGLY UNSTOPPABLE OTTOMANS HAD ALMOST ERADICATED THE BYZANTINE EMPIRE.

Constantinople remained in Byzantine hands, but was already under siege from more than 100,000 troops led by Sultan Bayezid I. In response, Pope Boniface IX called for a new Crusade, and gradually an army was assembled. This consisted of roughly 10,000 Burgundians (led by John of Nevers), 1000 English, 6000 Germans and a massive force of about 60,000 Hungarians, ruled by Sigismund. The mainly Franco-Hungarian army had gathered in Buda by July 1396. Sigismund, who had direct experience of fighting the Ottomans, advised that the Crusaders should wait for the Turks to fight a defensive battle. However, the French compelled the army to advance on the city of Nicoplis to the south, and besiege the Ottomans there.

WAITING TO ATTACK

The French idea was to draw the Turks into battle through their attempt to relieve Nicopolis, and this much went to plan. Bayezid ➤➤

Sigismund was crowned king of Hungary on 31 March 1387, and within only two years of his coronation he was forced to fight against Turkish invasion. Here he holds a war conference in Buda with the allies.

Above: An Ottoman cavalryman. This cavalry included mounted archers as well as lancers, both outfitted in chain armour as illustrated here.

Right: The unimaginative linearity of crusader tactics is apparent here, while the Turks relied more on encirclement and ambush.

drew off men from Constantinople, combined them with a large Allied force from Serbia, and arrived at Nicopolis on 24 September with around 104,000 men. The battle lines were drawn.

FATAL PURSUIT

The Crusaders created a vanguard of French and English cavalry, supported by three huge blocks of Hungarian troops further back. Again ignoring Sigismund's caution, the French and English cavalry charged, but were pulled to a halt by a line of defensive stakes. Under showers of Turkish arrows, the knights dismounted and cleared the stakes, before driving back the Ottoman lines and killing around 15,000 enemy. The Crusaders pushed the Turks over the brow of a hill, only to discover that on the other side was the bulk of the Ottoman army, which then attacked in force.

The French cavalry was completely destroyed, and seeing this, elements of the Hungarian force began to retreat. However, Sigismund took the mass of his army against the Ottomans, and seemed to be making headway until the bulk of Serbian forces, under Stefan Lazarevic, joined the battle. The Crusading army finally collapsed, with Sigismund fleeing and John of Nevers captured. The crushing defeat meant that it was effectively the last Crusade of the Middle Ages. ∎

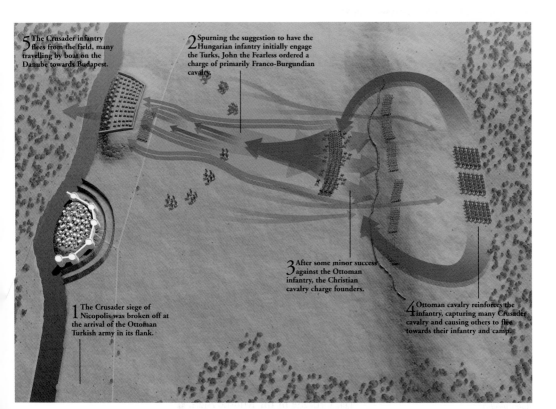

5 The Crusader infantry flees from the field, many travelling by boat on the Danube towards Budapest.

2 Spurning the suggestion to have the Hungarian infantry initially engage the Turks, John the Fearless ordered a charge of primarily Franco-Burgundian cavalry.

3 After some minor success against the Ottoman infantry, the Christian cavalry charge founders.

4 Ottoman cavalry reinforces the infantry, capturing many Crusader cavalry and causing others to flee towards their infantry and camp.

1 The Crusader siege of Nicopolis was broken off at the arrival of the Ottoman Turkish army in its flank.

BATTLE OF TANNENBERG

BY THE BEGINNING OF THE FIFTEENTH CENTURY, THE MILITARY MONASTIC ORDER OF THE TEUTONIC KNIGHTS WAS AT THE HEIGHT OF ITS POWER.

In 1400, the Knights' territory, known as the Ordenland, covered what became Prussia and present-day Latvia and Estonia. Ruling from their castle at Marienberg, the Knights governed the subject peoples with both Bible and sword, conducting violent raids into Lithuanian territory to gain converts and booty. In 1409, a revolt of the Samogitian tribe against the Order spiralled into a larger military crisis when Poland, Lithuania and Russia (here referred to as the 'union') combined arms against the powerful Knights.

> **KEY FACTS**
>
> **14 July 1410** – Teutonic Order suffers a crushing defeat at the height of its power, inflicted by a combined Polish-Lithuanian-Russian army at Tannenberg.
>
> **Teutonic knights** and infantry ultimately unable to stop the last of a series of union cavalry charges, and loses 32,000 troops.

AMBUSHED

The Order responded by forming up an army of around 80,000 men, commanded by Grand Master of the Teutonic Order, Ulrich von Jungingen. Of these, 20,000 were mounted knights. One hundred cannon created an artillery unit, and Swiss and English mercenaries filled out the ranks of the infantry. After an initial shift of position, the Order army took up battle positions between the villages of Tannenberg and Lodwigowo, with infantry and artillery forming the first two ranks and the elite cavalry massing behind. On 14 July, the union forces closed up with the Order's army and battle began. ➤➤

At Tannenberg, the Teutonic Knights – although extremely capable warriors – were simply unable to break the enemy ranks and wore themselves against the battle lines until they exposed themselves to an attack from the rear.

Jungingen initiated the battle with a bombardment from his 100 cannon, although in these early days of gunpowder warfare the weapons were capable of little more than creating a deafening noise. The artillery force was then overrun by Tartar cavalry, the situation only being restored by the charge of the Order knights.

DESTRUCTION OF THE ORDER

Now the opposing infantries clashed in a brutal action, and a Lithuanian cavalry charge was again broken by the knights, who began pursuing fleeing union troops into nearby marshland. However, many of the knights were killed here by an ambush from hidden Lithuanian troops. Furthermore, Russian forces in the centre lines held firm, and suddenly the Polish cavalry took advantage of a sudden lull in combat to cut deep into the Order ranks, while other Lithuanian units assaulted around against the enemy rear. Disaster was looming for the Order. Jungingen was dragged off his horse and killed. He had already given the order for withdrawal, but around 32,000 troops were lost – dead, wounded or captured in the rout. Following the defeat, the Teutonic Order went into a decline from which it never recovered. ■

The Teutonic Knights were a curious mixture of Christian piety and a high standard of martial expertise.

AGINCOURT

THE SCALE OF THE MILITARY TRIUMPH FOR ENGLAND AT THE BATTLE OF AGINCOURT IN 1415 TENDS TO OVERSHADOW THE MAGNITUDE OF DISASTER EXPERIENCED THERE BY FRANCE.

So much was to the French advantage. First, the English army under Henry V had been campaigning in France since 13 August 1415, and by October 1415 it had been reduced to a force not exceeding 6000 men, with many of them weakened by disease or wounds. In this condition, the enemy was retreating back to Calais to re-equip. By contrast, the French deployed at least 25,000 men, and their commander, Constable Charles d'Albret, placed them across the path of English retreat at Agincourt in northern France. The English would now have to fight.

SHOWER OF ARROWS

The date was 25 October 1415. The battlefield was a section of ploughed land about 730m (2394ft) wide, sited between two woods (one at Agincourt; the other at Tramecourt). D'Albret placed his forces across the northern end of land, which, crucially, had recently been drenched with rain. Confident that the three-to-one disparity ➤➤

The English army at Agincourt was much depleted by weeks of campaigning and exposure to the elements.

Above: The battle of Agincourt has gone into the realms of British legend, immortalized through art and Shakespeare's Henry V.
Right: The diagram here shows the dispositions of French and English forces, but cannot represent the hard walking conditions presented by the freshly ploughed terrain.

in numbers would carry the day, d'Albret launched two inadequate cavalry charges, aiming to break open Henry's line of archers and infantry. Instead, they were cut to ribbons by English arrows, and were forced to fall back, crashing straight into the 8000 French men-at-arms that had now been deployed in a foot assault.

RAINING ARROWS

The French soldiers made tortuous headway across the muddy field, struck down in the clouds of arrows, and so tightly packed across the field that they were unable to deploy their weapons properly. D'Albret simply added more troops, which actually made the situation even worse, while curiously not making use of his own archers and crossbowmen, who could have reversed the impending defeat.

A brief bright moment occurred for the French when an attack around the rear threatened the English camp, but this was fought off and Henry ordered the massacre of hundreds of French prisoners already taken, in case they should be tempted to rebel. When the final collapse came, it was total. D'Albret was dead, as were about 8000 Frenchmen, including 5000 nobles. English casualties were around 400 men. It was a disaster for the French, which augured the end of the age of chivalry. ■

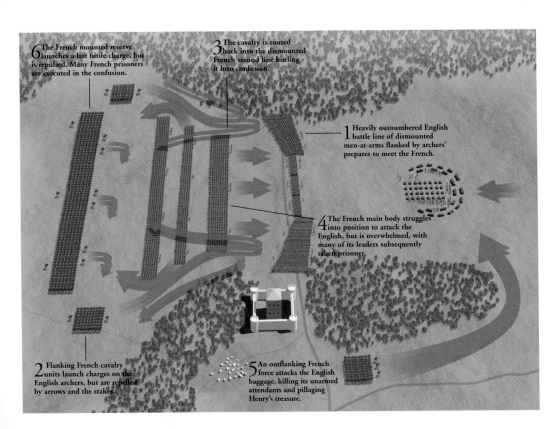

6 The French mounted reserve launches a last futile charge, but is repulsed. Many French prisoners are executed in the confusion.

3 The cavalry is routed back into the dismounted French second line hurling it into confusion.

1 Heavily outnumbered English battle line of dismounted men-at-arms flanked by archers' prepares to meet the French.

4 The French main body struggles into position to attack the English, but is overwhelmed, with many of its leaders subsequently taken prisoner.

2 Flanking French cavalry units launch charges on the English archers, but are repelled by arrows and the stakes.

5 An outflanking French force attacks the English baggage, killing its unarmed attendants and pillaging Henry's treasure.

FALL OF CONSTANTINOPLE

SINCE THE FOURTH CENTURY AD, THE POWERFUL CITY OF CONSTANTINOPLE HAD BEEN AN ARAB OBJECTIVE.

In 1453, it was the turn of the Ottoman empire under Sultan Mehmet II to attempt to take the Christian bastion. The defenders of the city would be heavily outnumbered by the Ottoman Turks; however, they were capable of putting out heavy volumes of arrows, crossbow bolts and artillery shot from the city's battlements, and were well protected behind walls that were several metres thick in places. This time, however, the walls would not be enough to keep the enemy at bay.

OUTGUNNED

On 2 April 1453, the Ottomans began wrapping the city with up to 100,000 troops, the siege being completed several days later. The Turks had brought with them huge siege cannon created by the legendary Hungarian gun founder Urban, some of the weapons having bores of 76cm (30in): Tragically, Urban's previous dealings had been with the Byzantines, but he had switched sides to the Ottomans after a dispute over wages. The ➤➤

KEY FACTS

April 2, 1453 – Ottoman forces begin besieging the city of Constantinople.

Ottomans use superior artillery technology to breach Constantinople's walls.

29 May – Ottoman infantry assaults breach the city's defences and Constantinople falls, the Ottomans extracting a terrible vengeance on the city's population.

An engraving depicting the conquest of Constantinople by the Turks.

Above: The Ottomans demonstrated highly developed siegecraft.
Right: The unfolding siege.

shells fired from Urban's guns soon had a traumatic impact upon the city walls and their defenders, and the citizens found themselves engaged in constant and frantic battle-damage repairs. Worse still, Constantinople's gunpowder reserves ran out in May, meaning that the defenders were no longer able to put out the harassing fire which had at least limited the Ottoman bombardments.

SIEGE WARFARE

Massed – and at first suicidal – Ottoman infantry attacks began on the city on 29 May. Initially, the defenders were able to repel the attacks, but their strength soon waned. After 55 days of siege, and during the third major infantry assault (this time by the Ottoman Janissaries, the Turks' most professional soldiers), the city's walls were breached and the enemy flooded into the interior. Thousands of Constantinople's inhabitants were put to the sword, and equal numbers of women were raped or enslaved. Had they invested in artillery in the same way as the Ottomans, the Byzantines might have been able to resist their fate. As it was, the great centre of eastern Christianity fell to what was rapidly becoming one of the most powerful empires on earth. ∎

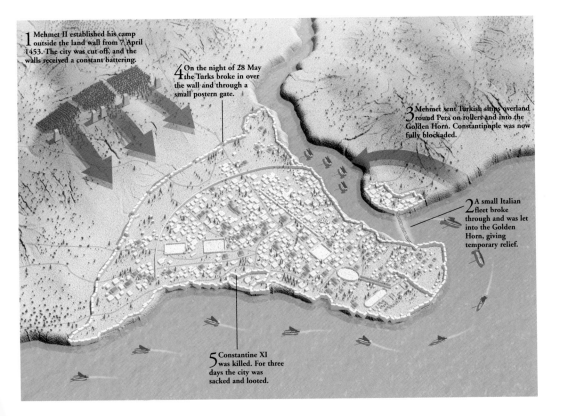

1 Mehmet II established his camp outside the land wall from 7 April 1453. The city was cut off, and the walls received a constant battering.

4 On the night of 28 May the Turks broke in over the wall and through a small postern gate.

3 Mehmet sent Turkish ships overland round Pera on rollers and into the Golden Horn. Constantinople was now fully blockaded.

2 A small Italian fleet broke through and was let into the Golden Horn, giving temporary relief.

5 Constantine XI was killed. For three days the city was sacked and looted.

NANCY

THE BATTLE OF NANCY IN 1477 WAS THE LAST MILITARY DISASTER PRESIDED OVER BY CHARLES THE BOLD OF BURGUNDY.

Charles had illusions of military greatness undermined by reality. The previous year, he had suffered two disastrous defeats at Grandson and Morat, both against the elite forces of the Swiss Federation. Learning little, and controlling a demoralized Burgundian/mercenary army of around 8000 men, he once again met the Swiss on 5 January 1477 at Nancy, the capital of Lorraine.

FORCED ON THE DEFENSIVE

Charles's objective was to recapture Nancy from Duc Réné of Lorraine, who had taken the city in 1476. Charles advanced and placed Nancy under siege from October 1476. His under-resourced troops suffered terribly from winter injuries such as frostbite and hypothermia (some 400 troops died of the cold on 24 December alone). In response to the siege, Réné directed an army of at least 20,000 men – including 8000 feared Swiss pikemen – to break the siege. Charles went on the defensive. He positioned his troops in a wooded valley to Nancy's south, hoping to force Réné's units into a narrow front that would break up the Swiss phalanxes. Furthermore, Charles positioned archers, handgunners and mounted knights on his flanks, his overall battle plan imitative of those used by Edward III. ➤➤

KEY FACTS

October 1476 – Charles the Bold of Burgundy besieges the city of Nancy with a force of 8000 troops.

5 January 1477 – Charles fights against a 20,000-strong relief force commanded by Réné of Lorraine.

Charles is hopelessly outflanked by the enemy and his army destroyed, 7000 men dying. He was himself killed by a Swiss halberdier.

The tomb of Charles the Bold of Burgundy. Charles earned his nickname on account of his impetuous bravery. Although a generally poor military commander, he was nonetheless also a capable administrator and governor.

➤➤

PERSONAL DISASTER

As had happened on so many previous occasions, Charles the Bold of Burgundy's ideas failed under the test of reality. The Swiss had rigorously scouted the Burgundian positions and, instead of being drawn up the valley, launched two major flanking attacks through the forest. A force of 7000 Swiss infantry and 2000 cavalry overthrew Charles's left flank and destroyed his artillery (Charles had 30 cannon positioned to the front). At the same time, Charles's right flank began to collapse under an assault by 8000 infantry and 1300 cavalry.

The jaws of the Swiss trap closed, and Charles desperately tried to restore the situation through sheer personal will. However, a Swiss halberdier split open Charles's head from his crown to his chin, and his army ultimately went down with 7000 dead. Charles's body was not discovered until three days later, dismembered, frozen and eaten by animals. ■

The parliament of Charles the Bold is here seen in session. Charles ruled his kingdom strongly, and his death brought about the fragmentation of Burgundy.

An artistic impression of Charles the Bold of Burgundy's last moments, as he is struck down by a Swiss halberdier.

BATTLE OF BOSWORTH

IN 1485, THE THRONE OF ENGLAND WAS BEING CONTESTED BY TWO PRINCIPALS, THE LANCASTRIAN HENRY TUDOR (RECENTLY RETURNED FROM EXILE IN FRANCE) AND THE YORKIST RICHARD III.

Henry had built up a composite army of around 5000 men, including 2000 mercenaries taken from France and other troops gathered during a recruitment trip through Wales. He then took his force from Milford Haven in South Wales and crossed back into England to meet with Richard. As the two sides closed towards battle around the Leicestershire town of Market Bosworth, however, it was Richard who had cause for confidence.

RELUCTANT ALLIES

Through bribery and political coercion, Richard had constructed a force in excess of 10,000 men. Richard had even kidnapped the son of Sir Thomas Stanley to force Stanley's additional contribution of 3000 troops, alongside a similar-sized force from Thomas's brother, Sir William Stanley. On 21 August, prior to the arrival of the Stanleys' troops, Richard ranked his force in three 'battles' (equivalent to divisions) on or near the salient ground of ➤➤

KEY FACTS

22 August 1485 – Henry's army of 5000 defeats a 10,000-strong force of Richard III.

Richard betrayed by the forces of the Stanley nobles, which switch sides mid-battle.

Richard killed, his mutilated body thrown into a nearby marsh.

The fighting at Bosworth Field was bloody and bitter, and did not spare Richard. He was dragged down from his horse, and once he was upon the ground Welsh infantry impaled him on pikes and smashed his armour in with axes.

Above: A marker stands on the site of the battle of Bosworth Field showing the spot where Richard III died, the king having fought a desperate battle for survival after being dismounted from his horse. The death of Richard inaugurated the Tudor period of the British monarchy.

Ambien Hill. The Stanleys' forces arrived the next day and, crucially, positioned themselves off to the sides of the battlefield, rather than join Richard's main force.

THE KILLING OF RICHARD

Bosworth was to be Richard's military disaster, mainly through political miscalculation rather than military ineptitude. On 22 August, Henry's army squared up to Richard's, and battle began with a charge by the cavalry of the Duke of Norfolk, fighting for Richard, against Henry's right flank commanded by the Earl of Oxford. In the ensuing melee, Richard spotted a bewildered Henry and his bodyguard separated from his main force. Richard charged, and he began hacking his way through to his competitor backed by around 1500 knights. At that moment, the Stanleys showed their true political colours and charged against Richard's force. Richard's flank was turned, and he was surrounded and battered to death by infantry. Richard's army was crushed; Henry became King Henry VII. Ironically, it was Richard's very political menace that brought military collapse from what should have been a straightforward victory. ■

Richard's disaster on Bosworth Field owes as much to the treachery of his allies as to tactical conditions. His chief betrayer, Lord Stanley, actually crowned Henry Tudor on the battlefield following the king's death.

EARLY MODERN DISASTERS
1500 – 1759

The refinement of gunpowder weapons, the birth of huge standing armies and the political infighting of the age made the Early Modern period replete with military triumph and disaster. At the battle of Nagashino (1575) some 3000 matchlock-armed infantry inflicted almost 70 per cent casualties on the samurai siege forces of Takeda Katsuyori. The battle of Blenheim saw the French suffer 31,000 casualties out of an army of 60,000. Such huge casualty figures became commonplace, and presaged the forthcoming industrial-scale warfare that would blight the world in the twentieth century.

Left: The Battle of Blenheim in 1704 saw troops killed by
ball, shot and sword and also drowning.

FLODDEN

IN 1513, JAMES IV OF SCOTLAND MADE A CRITICAL STRATEGIC BLUNDER BY INVADING ENGLAND.

England's king Henry VIII was away conducting his own invasion of France, and the moment may well have appeared propitious for James's southern ambitions. James took a large army (of possibly around 50,000 men) across the border into Northumberland in August, and made some initial gains, taking minor castles at Norham and Werk.

OVERWHELMING FIREPOWER

The English response came mainly from Thomas Howard, Earl of Surrey, who marched north to face James with an army of roughly 20,000 men. At Flodden near Branxton, Northumberland, James took up position on high ground bordered by the River Till. He missed an opportunity to repeat William Wallace's victory at Stirling Bridge, when the English had been forced to cross the Till across the narrow Twizel Bridge. Surrey was allowed to cross unimpeded, despite the Scottish guns being trained on the bridge, and he formed up his army into two large divisions. ➤➤

A scene of Edinburgh in the traumatic aftermath of the Scottish defeat at Flodden.

On the afternoon of 9 September, the Scottish forces began the attack. An initial exchange of cannon proved to the English advantage, as the Scottish gunners were frequently unable to depress their muzzles enough to engage the English accurately. English cannon fire began to rip open the Scottish ranks, as did the clouds of arrows being fired by the English archers. Having finally had enough, the Scottish force descended from the high ground at a charge.

BROKEN RANKS

The journey down the slippery hillside broke up the Scottish formations. Nevertheless, the Scots were still able to make some devastating incisions into English lines, led by James himself. Yet an unexpected attack up Branxton Hill by the English left flank under Sir Edward Stanley ejected James's reserve, and suddenly James's soldiers found themselves trapped. Stanley's forces now attacked James's rear, and the Scots were decimated in bloody hand-to-hand fighting.

James himself was cut down, along with an estimated 10,000 of his men. The disaster still resonates in Scottish memory today, and is recounted in the 'Flowers of the Forest' ballad. ■

The destruction of the Scottish forces at Flodden was a disastrous end to James IV's England campaign. James relied on heavy artillery and pikemen armed with heavy pikes, but both were not suited to the terrain.

LEPANTO

IN 1570 THE OTTOMAN TURKS WERE REACHING THE ZENITH OF THEIR POWER, AND IN AUGUST OF THAT YEAR THEY TOOK ANOTHER TERRITORY, CYPRUS.

The capture of Cyprus, a Venetian possession, demonstrated the Ottomans' impressive naval capabilities – they had used 1116 galleys to transport 50,000 troops to the island. The extension of Turkish power throughout the Mediterranean seemed assured.

OUTMODED TACTICS

In response to the fall of Cyprus, Pope Pius V ordered the creation of a Holy League naval force, a fleet of around 210 ships put together by Venice and other Italian states, as well as Malta, Genoa, Spain and various Habsburg countries. Commanded by Don Juan of Austria, the Holy League vessels set sail for Cyprus. Sultan Selim, the Ottoman ruler, dispatched almost his entire war fleet to deal with the threat – a total of 275 galleys. Ottoman naval tactics revolved around close-range archery fire, ramming and boarding, and the tactics seemed justified by the fact that the Ottomans had not experienced a serious battle defeat for ➤➤

KEY FACTS

7 October 1571 – Ottoman fleet of 275 vessels is defeated by the 210 ships of the Holy League.

Although the Holy League fleet was smaller, it heavily outgunned the Ottomans in terms of cannon.

The Ottomans lost 200 ships, the greatest loss of vessels in a single engagement in naval warfare.

Although Lepanto was a naval battle, it frequently had little to distinguish it from a land battle. Aboard one ship, the Reale, *around 400 Spanish arquebusiers were firing volleys from the deck into the Turkish sailors.*

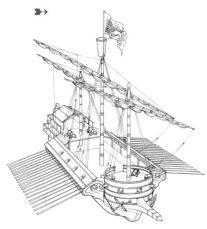

Above: The galleas was the most powerful combat vessel among the Holy League fleet at Lepanto. It was a hybrid form of galley equipped with increased cannon armament and castles (raised deck sections to fore and aft).

Right: Although Lepanto did feature tactical manoeuvres, the battle was mainly a slugging match.

around 200 years. However, the approaching European fleet had switched its emphasis to firepower, and, despite having fewer ships, it still outgunned the Ottomans by 1815 cannon to the Ottomans' 750. The Holy League also had six new galleass vessels, with formidable broadside batteries and frontally mounted cannon.

NAVAL BATTLE

The fleets closed for battle around Lepanto off the Greek coast on 7 October 1571. The Ottoman ships were powered mainly by slave rowers, who drove the Turkish ships in among the enemy vessels, to be met by ripples of gunfire, which they could not match. It soon became apparent that the Ottoman navy was outdated. In the resulting gun battle, during which the Ottoman ships eventually ran out of gunpowder, a total of 200 Ottoman vessels were either sunk or captured, a catastrophic loss. By contrast, the Holy League lost only 15 vessels. To their credit, the Ottomans rebuilt their navy along more modern lines following the defeat, but the myth of Ottoman invincibility had been emphatically laid to rest. ■

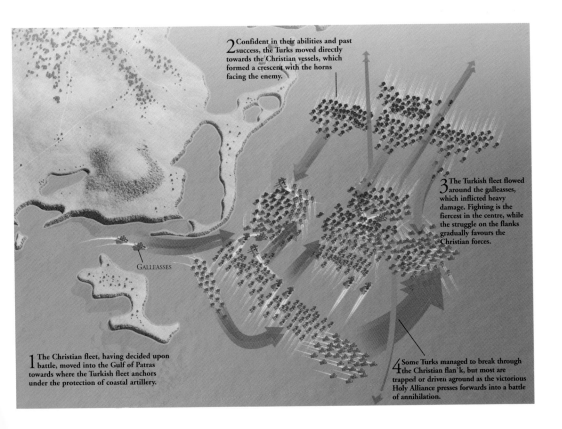

2 Confident in their abilities and past success, the Turks moved directly towards the Christian vessels, which formed a crescent with the horns facing the enemy.

3 The Turkish fleet flowed around the galleasses, which inflicted heavy damage. Fighting is the fiercest in the centre, while the struggle on the flanks gradually favours the Christian forces.

GALLEASSES

1 The Christian fleet, having decided upon battle, moved into the Gulf of Patras towards where the Turkish fleet anchors under the protection of coastal artillery.

4 Some Turks managed to break through the Christian flank, but most are trapped or driven aground as the victorious Holy Alliance presses forwards into a battle of annihilation.

BATTLE OF NAGASHINO

THE BATTLE OF NAGASHINO WAS A MILITARY DISASTER RESULTING FROM AN ELITE FORCE MEETING SUPERIOR TECHNOLOGY.

In 1575, the army of Takeda Katsuyori was besieging Nagashino castle in central Japan, part of the regular wars for samurai ascendancy during the sixteenth century. Takeda, who commanded a well-trained army of around 15,000 men, had an excellent military pedigree, being the son of the late Takeda Shingen, one of Japan's foremost generals.

HISTORY'S FIRST GUN BATTLE

After failing to take the castle, Takeda opted for siege to starve out the castle's inhabitants. However, a relief force of 38,000 men was raised, led by Oda Nobunaga and Tokugawa Ieyasu, and it advanced towards the castle to meet Takeda on the Shidarahara plain. The plain itself was crossed by the river Rengogawa, and the relief forces built a wooden barrier system behind the river to break up a cavalry charge, then took up positions further back.

Deciding that attack was the best defence, Takeda left behind 3000 men at the siege and took 12,000 of his soldiers out onto ➤➤

The samurai warrior's superb swordsmanship served him poorly in the face of emerging firearms technologies.

the plain. On 26 June 1575, at 6 a.m., Takeda launched a charge of his elite samurai horsemen and infantry.

VOLLEY FIRE

The charge slowed to negotiate the Rengogawa, and at this point the fortunes of the battle turned against Takeda. Oda's army included 3000 men armed with matchlock guns, and they were securely positioned behind the wooden palisade. As Takeda's soldiers struggled across the river, the matchlock men opened up with concentrated volley fire at a range of around 50m (164ft). Although the weapons were individually inaccurate, in volley form they devastated the samurai attackers, who fell in their hundreds. Takeda was unable to close distance and cross the palisade while the firearms were being reloaded, and soldiers of the relief force now ventured out from behind their barricades to attack the weakened enemy. Furthermore, an Oda raiding party of around 3000 men had attacked the siege forces to the rear, and routed them. The battle went on for around eight hours until Takeda ordered a retreat. Having faced the first instance of gunpowder volley fire in history, Takeda was leaving behind 10,000 dead on the battlefield, a horrific casualty rate approaching 70 per cent. ∎

Above: The matchlock gun worked by dropping a smouldering cord (or match) onto an open pan of gunpowder, the resultant flash being channelled via a port to detonate the main charge contained in the barrel. Matchlocks were highly inaccurate and unreliable in damp weather conditions.

A portrait of the Japanese military leader, Tokugawa Ieyasu. Tokugawa is regarded as one of the 'great unifiers' of Japan and in 1603 became shogun of almost the entire country.

SPANISH ARMADA

BY 28 MAY 1588, THE DATE WHEN THE SPANISH ARMADA SET SAIL FROM LISBON FOR ENGLISH WATERS, THE ANGLO-SPANISH WAR (1585–1604) HAD ALREADY BEEN RAGING FOR THREE YEARS.

Caused by the religious clash between Elizabeth's Protestant England and Philip II's Catholic Spain, and by economic competition over the Americas, the war left Philip II seeking a decisive action to crush the English. He opted for outright invasion. From 1586, a plan was developed to make an amphibious invasion of England from the Spanish Netherlands, using the 30,000 men of the Spanish Army of Flanders, led by Alessandro Farnese, Duke of Parma. In support, a Spanish armada would be dispatched from Lisbon to defeat the English navy and create a safe passage for Parma's army in the English Channel.

KEY FACTS

- **28 May 1588** – 130 ships of the Spanish Armada set sail from Lisbon, part of a planned invasion force destined for England.
- **6 August** – the Armada is forced from anchorage around Calais by British action, and has to return to Spain by sailing around the entire British Isles.
- **Only 60** vessels make it back to Spain, most of the losses resulting from storms.

THE PERFECT STORM

The Armada finally set sail in May 1588, commanded by the Duke of Medina-Sidonia. Total strength was around 130 vessels (although only 40 of these were warships), which were manned by 3000 crew and held around 19,000 soldiers. The English fleet, under Baron Charles Howard and with Sir Francis Drake as second-in-command, was actually of a similar strength to the Spanish, but it had far better, ➤➤

It is noteworthy that the Spanish made harbours along the Spanish and Portuguese coastlines prepare to receive casualties and damaged ships – the Armada leaders knew full well the dangers of the British navy and the Channel weather.

and far more, long-range cannon. However, in many ways, the subsequent Spanish disaster was caused by the weather, not by warfare. The Armada was forced to go to port at La Coruña in northern Spain by offshore storms, and returned to sea only in July. It was sighted off Cornwall on 29 July, and the English navy subsequently launched a series of harrying actions, using its long-range gunnery, although neither side sustained any serious losses.

DRIVEN OFF COURSE

The Armada anchored off Calais on 6 August, waiting for the army in Flanders to assemble and embark. However, the British floated eight fireships into the Armada's ranks, forcing them to up anchor, and on 8 July three Spanish ships were sunk in battle off Gravelines. More seriously, prevailing westerly winds drove the Armada northwards into the North Sea. By this time, Parma's invasion had been called off, so the Armada ships were faced with a return journey to Spain, which took it on an anticlockwise route around the entire British Isles. The journey saw the Armada battered by autumn storms, which sunk many ships in the Atlantic or dashed them against the Scottish or Irish coastline. Seventy Spanish ships were lost between the departure from La Coruña and the return to Santander on the Bay of Biscay, at a cost of 15,000 dead. ■

Right: Once the Spanish had lost their formation through the disruptive actions of the British, they were unable to form up again into a coherent invasion force.

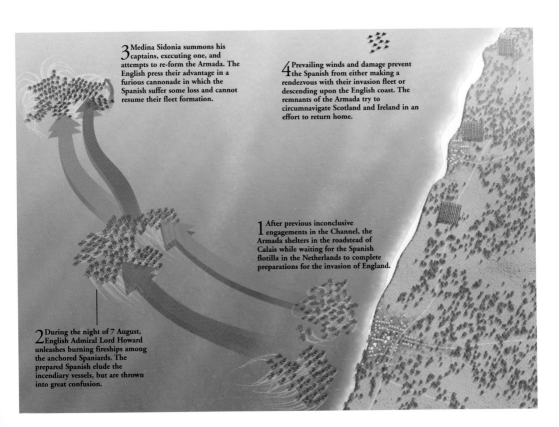

3 Medina Sidonia summons his captains, executing one, and attempts to re-form the Armada. The English press their advantage in a furious cannonade in which the Spanish suffer some loss and cannot resume their fleet formation.

4 Prevailing winds and damage prevent the Spanish from either making a rendezvous with their invasion fleet or descending upon the English coast. The remnants of the Armada try to circumnavigate Scotland and Ireland in an effort to return home.

1 After previous inconclusive engagements in the Channel, the Armada shelters in the roadstead of Calais while waiting for the Spanish flotilla in the Netherlands to complete preparations for the invasion of England.

2 During the night of 7 August, English Admiral Lord Howard unleashes burning fireships among the anchored Spaniards. The prepared Spanish elude the incendiary vessels, but are thrown into great confusion.

YELLOW FORD

IRELAND AT THE END OF THE SIXTEENTH CENTURY WAS A TROUBLED PLACE FOR THE ENGLISH.

During the reign of Elizabeth, the English had made numerous attempts to control and colonize the last Catholic stronghold of the British Isles, but the number of Irish revolts intensified in the second half of the century. The most troubling uprising began in 1594, when Hugh O'Neill, the Earl of Tyrone, created a large army of around 10,000 men, modernized their tactics and weaponry, and joined a rebellion that was to last until 1601.

THE ADVANCE HALTED

By 1598, O'Neill had inflicted several defeats upon the English, using classic Irish ambush and harassment tactics, and had even fought against his brother-in-law Marshal Sir Henry Bagenal (O'Neill had eloped with Bagenal's sister in 1591). The English lost patience. In the summer of 1598, O'Neill was besieging the Portmore Fortress on the Blackwater River, aiming to draw the English out into battle. He succeeded, and Henry Bagenal set out from Armagh to defeat his troublesome relative once and for all. ➺

KEY FACTS

14 August 1598 – 4000 English troops led by Sir Henry Bagenal to relieve a British fort on the Blackwater River are beseiged near Yellow Ford by the forces of Hugh O'Neill.

The Irish ambush the English column, and overwhelm it with musket fire and an infantry charge.

Bagenal and 2000 English troops are killed, the worst English defeat on Irish soil.

Irish rebel infantry, like the warriors of Scotland, used their knowledge of local terrain to advantage against the English forces, who at this time were ill suited to dealing with ambush and guerrilla-style warfare.

Above: The Irish rebel leader, Hugh O'Neill. O'Neill's rebellion in Ireland was particularly dangerous to the Protestant government of Elizabeth, as it had the backing of much of Catholic Europe.

The 4000 English troops heading towards Blackwater were well trained and well led, confident in their ability to overcome the Irish rebels. Furthermore, Irish supplies of musket, cannon and ammunition were running low, whereas the English brought with them large stocks of firepower.

BROKEN COLUMNS

On 14 August 1598, the English plan unravelled at a point called Yellow Ford, on the approaches to Blackwater River. Using both natural terrain and prepared earthworks, Irish infantry placed the English column under withering harassing fire along its flanks and its rear. Meanwhile, the English lead elements came up against a large ditch cut across the route of their advance. Irish fire also destroyed an English gunpowder wagon in a huge explosion that killed dozens. As the English formations collapsed into disorder, they were suddenly assaulted by a charge from thousands of Irish infantry. The confident advance had turned into total collapse. Bagenal, who had inadvisably taken up position at the front of his army, was killed along with around 2000 of his soldiers, the remainder surviving by taking sanctuary in Armagh cathedral. It was a terrible defeat for the English, and one which temporarily loosened their hold over Irish territory. ∎

O Sydney worthy of tryple renowne, For plagyng the traytours that troubled the crowne. 1581.

The early modern world saw constant friction and violence between England and Ireland, producing a dangerous political legacy that lasts to this day. Here Sir Henry Sidney, Lord Deputy of Ireland, returns to Dublin after a victory.

MAGDEBURG

THE SIEGE OF MAGDEBURG HAS GONE DOWN AS ONE OF THE MOST DREADFUL EPISODES OF THE THIRTY YEARS' WAR (1618–48).

In November 1630, an Imperial Catholic force was dispatched to take the northern German city of Magdeburg, known for its Lutheran tendencies. The Imperial force was commanded by General Gottfried Heinrich Graf zu Pappenheim. In the internecine Europe of the period, mercenaries filled out the ranks of many armies, the Imperial troops having their own hard core of degenerate warriors. In March 1631, the siege force was expanded by the addition of troops under the Catholic League's army commander, Johann Tserclaes, count of Tilly. The total forces surrounding Magdeburg now numbered around 22,000.

WANTON DESTRUCTION

Inside the city walls of Magdeburg were its citizens, plus a small holding force of Swedish infantry commanded by Colonel Dietrich von Falkenberg. Falkenberg concentrated on improving the city's defensive outworks as much as possible, and morally fortifying his soldiers, but of far greater concern was the nature of the civilian population. While Tilly and Pappenberg's siege cannon battered down the city's outer redoubts one by ➤

KEY FACTS

November 1630 – an Imperial Catholic siege army is sent to take Magdeburg, expanding to a 22,000-strong force by March 1631.

May – the city's commander, Colonel Dietrich von Falkenberg, pulls all his troops back inside the city walls and destroys the city's bridge over the Elbe.

20 May – a final Imperial assault takes the city, and 25,000 soldiers and civilians die in the subsequent slaughter.

Victorious Imperial forces advance through the ruined city of Magdeburg. It is testimony to the resilience of the city's fortifications that, even with a fearful and divided population, the city maintained its resistance for several months.

➡

one, Magdeburg's population vacillated between surrender and defiance, with the black-and-white options coloured to many different shades of grey by the various religious groups within the city, which included Catholics. Falkenberg, seeing an impending military collapse, destroyed the bridge over the river Elbe which led into the city, burnt down the suburbs, and pulled all soldiers back inside the city walls.

TOTAL DESTRUCTION

With no salvation in sight, Falkenberg was forced to give consideration to an ultimatum received from Tilly – surrender or face destruction. Yet even while Magdeburg's councils were debating the response, Tilly launched an all-out attack on the city on 20 May. With the defenders weak and vacillating, the determined storming soon broke through the city's walls, and the sacking of Magdeburg began. Fuelled by lust for booty and the desire to punish the city's occupants, the Imperial troops commenced a hideous massacre of the inhabitants. The city was also set on fire, resulting in a huge conflagration.

A total of 25,000 of Magdeburg's inhabitants were killed, either by the sword or by the fire, the remaining 5000 being mainly women, who were shipped off for a life of slavery. The sack of Magdeburg was an unparalleled disaster during the period, but it galvanized Protestant resistance through Europe (see next entry, the battle of Breitenfeld). ■

MAGDEBURG.

ALBIS   FLUVIUS

Die Elbe Flus

Magdeburg was an enormous challenge for the besieging Imperial forces; however, by 1630, siege cannon had reached a high level of practicality and more mobile wheeled field cannon had also been introduced.

BREITENFELD

IN MANY WAYS, THE BATTLE OF BREITENFELD WAS THE PROTESTANT
CORRECTIVE TO THE MASSACRE AT MAGDEBURG ON 20 MAY 1631
(SEE PREVIOUS ENTRY).

Following their victory at Magdeburg, the Imperial Catholic
forces took Leipzig without a struggle on 15 September. However,
they now faced a new threat from the advancing 35,000-strong
Swedish-Saxon army led by the militarily astute king of Sweden,
Gustavus Adolphus. Gustavus was heading to retake Leipzig, but
the two sides met about 8km (5 miles) to the north on the plain
of Leipzig, near the village of Breitenfeld.

UNDERPOWERED BUT MOBILE

The leader of the Imperial army, the Count of Tilly, was cautious
of his foe; however, Imperial confidence was running high. The
Catholics outnumbered Gustavus' army by around 6000 men, and
had ranked up their infantry in huge 2000-man battalion squares, packed with musket and pike.
By contrast, the Swedish-Saxon troops appeared thinly spread, the infantry only six ranks deep and
interspersed with cannon rather than having the great concentrations of firepower in the Imperial
lines. Yet Tilly and his leading general, Gottfried Heinrich Graf zu Pappenheim, could not see that ➤➤

KEY FACTS

17 September 1631 – a
Swedish-Saxon army and a
larger Catholic Imperialist
army meet in battle near
Breitenfeld, near Leipzig.

Imperialists threaten an
envelopment, but the
Swedish troops under
Gustavus Adolphus escape
the trap through manoeuvre.

The Imperialists are trapped by
a swinging, flanking attack,
and are defeated, with more
than 14,000 dead, wounded
or captured.

Gustavus Adolphus, here seen giving commands on the battlefield at Breitenfeld, treated his soldiers well in terms of clothing, training, medical services and pay, and so commanded a loyal and efficient force.

Above: Johan Tzerclas, the count of Tilly, is wounded at Breitenfeld. He would be killed in battle the following year, his opponent again the victorious Gustavus Adolphus.

Right: The battle of Breitenfeld was a tactically fluid one, with both sides attempting outflanking manoeuvres.

Gustavus was about to demonstrate the superiority of manoeuvrable firepower over large, unwieldy formations.

OUTMANOEUVRED

The battle began on the morning of 17 September 1631, Tilly launching a thunderous artillery barrage, but the stretched enemy lines meant that it was not decisive. By contrast, the Swedish artillery balls tumbled through rank after rank of Imperial troops, causing hideous casualties. Pappenheim on the left now charged with 5000 cavalry, while Tilly led an infantry/cavalry assault towards the right against the weaker Saxon units. It looked as if the Imperialists might achieve a classic envelopment. However, as Pappenheim's cavalry circled around the right flank, it discovered that it had actually been trapped between the enemy's front ranks and a hidden reserve. It was now decimated in crossfire of musket ball and grape shot. Also, redeployments had secured Gustavus' right flank, and his left flank now hinged across the battlefield like a huge door, taking the Imperial right flank and using its cannon to fire along the lines for maximum destruction. The Imperial troops fell apart, and before nightfall Gustavus had taken the battlefield. Although more than 4000 Swedish-Saxon troops had died, the Imperialists had lost 7600 men, with a similar numbered captured. ■

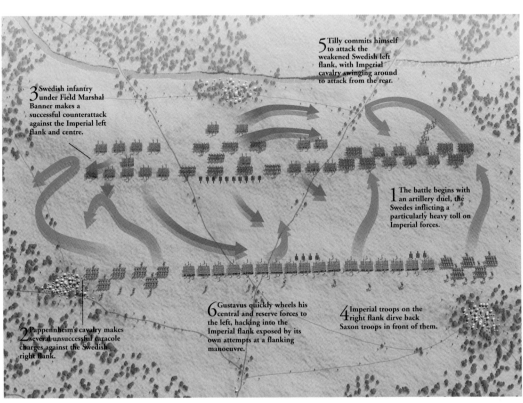

3 Swedish infantry under Field Marshal Banner makes a successful counterattack against the Imperial left flank and centre.

5 Tilly commits himself to attack the weakened Swedish left flank, with Imperial cavalry swinging around to attack from the rear.

1 The battle begins with an artillery duel, the Swedes inflicting a particularly heavy toll on Imperial forces.

2 Pappennheim's cavalry makes several unsuccessful caracole charges against the Swedish right flank.

6 Gustavus quickly wheels his central and reserve forces to the left, hacking into the Imperial flank exposed by its own attempts at a flanking manoeuvre.

4 Imperial troops on the right flank dirve back Saxon troops in front of them.

BLENHEIM

BY 1704, THE FRENCH ARMY HAD NOT EXPERIENCED A MAJOR DEFEAT FOR NEARLY HALF A CENTURY.

Its supremacy was finally destroyed at the battle of Blenheim on 13 August, part of the War of the Spanish Succession (1701–14). This brought to the field an Anglo-German-Dutch army of about 52,000 troops, led by the 1st Duke of Marlborough and Eugene of Savoy, against 60,000 Franco-Bavarian soldiers commanded by Marshal Camille, Comte de Tallard, Marsin and Maximillian II Emanuel, the Elector of Bavaria. The cause was a threatened Franco-Bavarian invasion of Austria, to crush the Grand Alliance formed against France. In response, Marlborough made a rapid, highly professional march from Koblenz to the river Danube.

SURPRISE ATTACK

Tallard now made a tactical mistake, assuming that the enemy would not attack directly, but instead take up defensive positions around Vienna. On 12 August, Marlborough and Eugene's forces combined on the Danube and drew the French into battle around the village of Blindheim (anglicized as Blenheim). ➤➤

KEY FACTS

12 August 1704 – an Anglo-German-Dutch army under Lord Marlborough surprises the French by deploying around Blenheim on the Danube.

13 August 1704 – the battle of Blenheim is fought, with 60,000 Franco-Bavarian troops resisting around 52,000 enemy soldiers.

The French centre weakens under assault, then collapses. The battle is lost with more than 30,000 casualties.

British cavalry makes a charge, its presence being decisive at the battle of Blenheim. John Churchill, 1st Duke of Marlborough, himself led several charges, distinguished by his pure white horse and conspicuous Order of the Garter.

The rapidity of the enemy appearance had unsettled the French, who deployed their forces poorly behind the river Nebel, stretched between Blenheim on the right flank and Lützingen on the left. The centre of the French line, controlled by Tallard himself, was particularly weak, relying almost entirely on cavalry.

BROKEN CENTRE

Battle began at 8.00 a.m. on 13 August with a French artillery barrage directed against the enemy on the other side of the Nebel. At 12.30 p.m., however, Marlborough's troops attacked across the length of the front. A holding attack by Eugene on the Allied right flank allowed Marlborough to cross the Nebel. Tallard responded with a cavalry counterattack, but this was blasted back by British gunfire. The French centre was now critically weakened, and at 5.30 p.m. it finally broke, allowing Marlborough to pour his men through and hinge left, trapping the French centre and right against the main width of the Nebel. The result was dreadful scenes of carnage among the French ranks, with those not killed by ball, shot or sword being drowned attempting to swim the Nebel. Blenheim itself (held by four regiments of dragoons) was surrendered at 11.00 p.m., by which time Tallard had been captured and some 31,000 of his troops had been killed, wounded or captured. ■

Right: The river Nebel, seen in this aerial view, formed a trap for the unfortunate French forces once they were thrown into retreat.

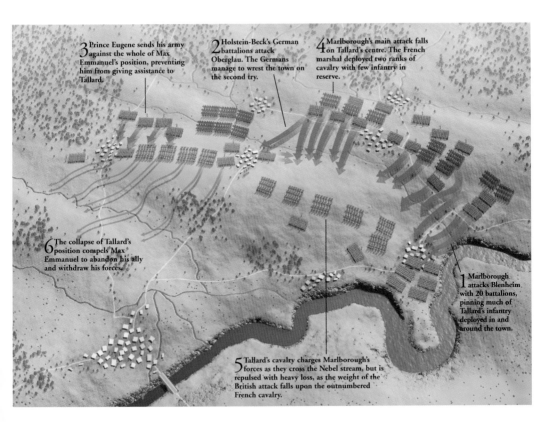

3 Prince Eugene sends his army against the whole of Max Emmanuel's position, preventing him from giving assistance to Tallard.

2 Holstein-Beck's German battalions attack Oberglau. The Germans manage to wrest the town on the second try.

4 Marlborough's main attack falls on Tallard's centre. The French marshal deployed two ranks of cavalry with few infantry in reserve.

6 The collapse of Tallard's position compels Max Emmanuel to abandon his ally and withdraw his forces.

1 Marlborough attacks Blenheim with 20 battalions, pinning much of Tallard's infantry deployed in and around the town.

5 Tallard's cavalry charges Marlborough's forces as they cross the Nebel stream, but is repulsed with heavy loss, as the weight of the British attack falls upon the outnumbered French cavalry.

CULLODEN

THE DEFEAT WHICH BEFELL THE REBELS AT CULLODEN IN 1746 WAS A BLOODY END TO THE JACOBITE UPRISING OF THE PREVIOUS YEAR.

The battle took place on 16 April at Culloden Field, near Inverness. On the one side was the Jacobite army of Charles Edward Stuart, who returned to Scotland from France in 1745 (bringing with him many French soldiers), then raised an army, intending to take the British throne. Facing him was the Duke of Cumberland, with a composite Hanoverian army of around 9000 men (including many Scots).

LOSING STRENGTH

In 1746, after a long campaign, the Jacobites were in the process of retreating back to Scotland, despite having threatened London itself in 1745. Exhausted and pursued by Cumberland's troops, they still had the strength to defeat the Hanoverians at Falkirk in January. By 16 April, however, when a further battle was fought at Culloden, the 5000 Jacobites were substantially outnumbered and outgunned by the Hanoverians. They were also short of supplies, the result being that men were forced to forage far afield and some ➤➤

KEY FACTS

16 April 1746 – around 5000 Jacobite rebels massacred by the 9000 Hanoverian soldiers of the Duke of Cumberland.

Many Jacobites killed in tightly packed lines by Hanoverian cannon and musket fire, the survivors being killed by English cavalry and infantry.

The Jacobite defeat signals the end of the Jacobite rebellion of 1745.

A scene from the battle of Culloden, as depicted by the Illustrated London News *some 100 years after the event. Jacobite broadswords were ultimately overwhelmed by British firepower and the bayonet.*

Above: Charles Stuart, following his defeat at Culloden, hid out in the Highlands before making his way to France. The rest of his life was one of descent into womanizing and alcohol. Having been expelled from France, he finally resided in Italy, dying in Rome in 1788.

took the opportunity to desert. On the 15th, Stuart's men had attempted an unsuccessful night attack on Cumberland's camp, so the 16th saw them form up on Culloden Field cold, tired and hungry. The landscape was also bordered by dykes, which had the effect of channelling the Jacobites into a tight target for the enemy cannon and musket.

ENGLISH FIREPOWER

The battle began, predictably enough, with devastating Hanoverian barrages, which ripped into the densely packed Jacobites. The Jacobites endured the slaughter in their lines for 20 minutes, then made a brave Highland charge at the opposing lines. Unfortunately, the boggy terrain disrupted the Jacobite ranks and made deploying muskets difficult, while the Hanoverian infantry flashed with coordinated musket fire. The enemy cavalry now swept through the Jacobite soldiers, and the infantry advanced to finish off the rebels. No prisoners were taken, the Hanoverian troops systematically slaughtering every Jacobite they found on the battlefield – although Charles Stuart escaped to France. 'I should have died on the field at Culloden,' he said. ∎

Jacobite leaders confer and recognize the failure of the rebellion begun in 1745.

ROSSBACH

THE DISASTER WHICH BEFELL THE FRANCO-IMPERIAL ALLIES AT THE BATTLE OF ROSSBACH IN 1757, WAS A CLASSIC EXAMPLE OF A LARGER FORCE BEING OUTMANOEUVRED BY A SMALLER FORCE.

The battle took place during the Seven Years' War, on 5 November 1757, near the village of Rossbach in Prussian Saxony.

TACTICS ANTICIPATED

Charles de Rohan, Prince de Soubrise, was in command of around 42,000 Imperial soldiers, who were seeking battle with some 21,000 Prussian troops commander by Frederick the Great. On 3 November, Frederick's army was encamped near Wendorf, but moved south on the 4th to take up defensive positions just north of Rossbach. Soubrise sensed the opportunity of a major victory, and, on the morning of the 5th, he started to move his massive force southwards in five huge columns, aiming to march around the Prussian left flank, take up positions west of Reichardtswerben, and make a northward assault into the outflanked enemy. However, deploying such a military mass took hours, and columns and regiments soon became mashed up in the giant manoeuvres. By ➤➤

KEY FACTS

5 November 1757 – Franco-Imperial army attempts to outflank a smaller Prussian army near the village of Rossbach.

Prussian forces outmanoeuvre the French-led Allies, and attack them from the east before they are fully prepared.

Allies are completely routed, with nearly 8000 losses for only 550 Prussian casualties.

Imperial and Prussian troops clash at the battle of Rossbach. Compared to the Prussian forces arraigned against them, the Franco-Imperial army suffered from a generally sluggish and unimaginative command-and-control system

Above: Frederick II of Prussia, also known as Frederick the Great, was raised by a strict, militaristic father who sometimes physically beat the young Frederick after making mistakes in tactical exercises.

Right: The map illustrates both the confusion in the Allied tactics and the brilliance of the Prussian manoeuvres.

contrast, Frederick – having deduced the French plan – mobilized his army in around 40 minutes. He took them around the concealing features known as Janus Hugel and Pölzen Hugel, and met the Franco-Imperial forces from the east with a rapid thrust from 38 squadrons of cavalry led by General von Seydlitz.

TACTICAL DEFEAT

The unwieldy Franco-Imperial columns had not entirely formed up properly, and their responses were chaotic. Furthermore, the French now came under attack by Prussian infantry from Janus Hugel itself. Soubrise sought to restore the situation through counterattack, but the Prussians had managed to site batteries of cannon in support of their infantry and the French bayonet charge was ripped apart by ball and grapeshot. Allied order now broke down completely, with most of the troops fleeing the field. When the final casualty lists were drawn up, it transpired that the Franco-Imperial force had lost 7700 men; despite having a two-to-one advantage over the enemy, it had managed to inflict only 550 casualties upon the Prussians. The only good thing to come out of the battle for the French was a major rethink of tactics, with a new understanding of the need for rapid manoeuvre rather than large, ponderous deployments. ∎

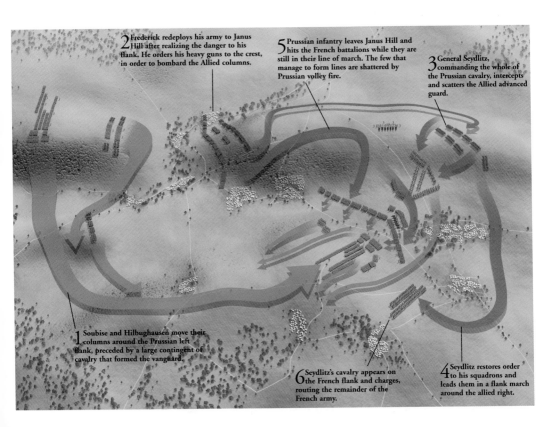

2 Frederick redeploys his army to Janus Hill after realizing the danger to his flank. He orders his heavy guns to the crest, in order to bombard the Allied columns.

5 Prussian infantry leaves Janus Hill and hits the French battalions while they are still in their line of march. The few that manage to form lines are shattered by Prussian volley fire.

3 General Seydlitz, commanding the whole of the Prussian cavalry, intercepts and scatters the Allied advanced guard.

1 Soubise and Hilbughausen move their columns around the Prussian left flank, preceded by a large contingent of cavalry that formed the vanguard.

6 Seydlitz's cavalry appears on the French flank and charges, routing the remainder of the French army.

4 Seydlitz restores order to his squadrons and leads them in a flank march around the allied right.

LEUTHEN

FREDERICK THE GREAT OF PRUSSIA WAS A MILITARY LEADER OF EXCEPTIONAL TALENT, YET SO MANY OF HIS VICTORIES WERE ASSISTED BY THE OVERCONFIDENCE AND TACTICAL CONSERVATISM OF HIS ENEMIES.

Such was the case at the battle fought around the village of Leuthen in Silesia. On 5 December 1757, the Prussians faced an 80,000-strong Austrian army led by Prince Charles of Lorraine.

MISDIRECTED REINFORCEMENTS

Considering that the Prussian army was only 36,000 men, the advantage immediately seemed to lie with the Austrians. Furthermore, Austrian defensive positions initially appeared good, with marshland protecting their northern flank and their being solid concentrations of artillery along the lines. However, Charles had overextended his lines – they measured 6.4km (4 miles) from Nippern to Schriegwitz, and hence were vulnerable to exactly the kind of oblique attack Frederick chose to employ. Moreover, the right flank had limited movement precisely because of the surrounding marshlands. ➤➤

KEY FACTS

5 December 1757 – An 80,000-strong Austrian army fights 36,000 Prussian troops under Frederick around the village of Leuthen, Silesia.

The Austrians become focused entirely on an attack against their right flank, and are thrown into disarray by a surprise assault against their left.

The Austrian army is defeated, with 27,000 casualties.

A vivid artwork depicting the intensity of the fighting around the village of Leuthen. The Prussian victory was yet another example of Frederick the Great's superb generalship.

Above: A Prussian hussar, here armed with a flintlock musket and a sabre. Hussar uniforms of most countries tended to be based on Hungarian national costume.

Right: The map illustrates the battle.

By late morning, the Austrians' right under General Lucchese was indeed facing an attack. The Austrians' first mistake was to treat this assault as the main threat, forgetting about their more vulnerable left flank. Lucchese asked Charles for reinforcements, and consequently Charles pulled away reserves from the left flank, diverting them northwards. Meanwhile, Frederick ordered a large force of infantry cavalry to right-turn at the village of Borne and advance downwards towards the enemy's left flank; its advance was partially hidden by high ground in the centre of the battlefield.

DISPROPORTIONATE CASUALTIES

Here the Austrians made the critical mistake of overconfidence. Charles and his second-in-command, Marshal Daun, interpreted this sudden manoeuvre of Prussian units as a sign that they were in retreat. Indeed, they mockingly described the manoeuvre as a 'changing of the guard'. However, Frederick's troops suddenly emerged to make an oblique attack on the Austrian left. Charles responded by wheeling his army to face south, but the stretched line moved inefficiently, and despite some vigorous Austrian counterattacks the Austrian forces were steadily crushed. Some 27,000 men were killed, wounded or captured, the cost to the Prussians being only around a quarter of that total. ∎

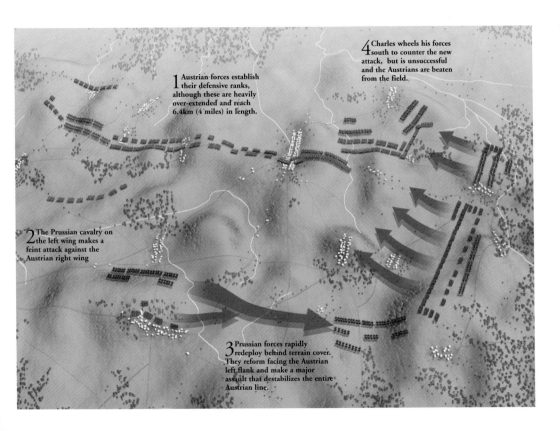

1 Austrian forces establish their defensive ranks, although these are heavily over-extended and reach 6.4km (4 miles) in length.

2 The Prussian cavalry on the left wing makes a feint attack against the Austrian right wing

3 Prussian forces rapidly redeploy behind terrain cover. They reform facing the Austrian left flank and make a major assault that destabilizes the entire Austrian line.

4 Charles wheels his forces south to counter the new attack, but is unsuccessful and the Austrians are beaten from the field.

MINDEN

THE BATTLE OF MINDEN WAS ONE OF THE MANY CLASHES THAT OCCURRED IN EUROPE DURING THE POLITICALLY TANGLED CONFLICT WHICH WAS THE SEVEN YEARS' WAR (1756–63).

The year was 1759, and a huge French force of up to 52,000 men led by Marshal de Contades had advanced into Westphalia and taken the city of Minden, and it was now threatening the Electorate of Hanover. To meet Contades and protect Hanover, Ferdinand of Brunswick marched out to battle with a 41,000-strong Anglo-Hanoverian army. Contades was in a strong position. Not only did his force numerically dominate the Allied troops heading against him, but he also had good defensive positions at Minden around the marshes of the Weser river.

MISCOMMUNICATION AND DISOBEDIENCE

Artillery exchanges between the two sides began at first light on the morning of 1 August 1759, followed by infantry clashes along the lines. There then occurred a mistake on the Allied part, which should have clinched the battle for the French. Ferdinand had a reserve force of nine infantry regiments under General Sporcken. ➨

KEY FACTS

1 August 1749 – French army of around 52,000 men meets an Anglo-Hanoverian army of 22,000 men around Minden in Westphalia.

French troops are broken apart when a misunderstanding among the Anglo-Hanoverians results in a large reserve column of infantry being sent straight into the French lines.

The French suffer an appalling defeat, with around 10,000 men dead.

The battle of Minden was an occasion when problems in Anglo-Hanoverian command and control actually aided in the defeat of the French forces. Orders had to be relayed by runner or signal, both of which could become easily lost in the smoke of battle.

After a command from Ferdinand was incorrectly relayed, Sporcken advanced against the French lines, taking his units out in column (often a suicidal formation in battle) and beyond the support of the Allied cavalry and artillery. Contades was amazed, and directed the fire of 60 cannon into the Allied mass, then launched an 11-squadron cavalry charge. To Contades' horror, however, his cavalry were cut off by musket fire and bayonet.

FRENCH DEFEAT

Unbeknown to Contades, the British general Lord George Sackville had disobeyed orders to deploy a cavalry charge to repel the French. The battle should have been going to the French, but this obstinate column fought off the French cavalry. Furthermore, the main body of Allied artillery and infantry had now caught up with Sporcken's troops, and after five hours of battle the French were routed. The French had lost up to 10,000 men against Allied losses of around 2500. Contades was dumbfounded at the fact that Sporcken's isolated column had carved into three lines of cavalry and four brigades of infantry, suffering 30 per cent casualties. What should have been Contades' victory, aided by Allied incompetence, turned into a major defeat through the obstinacy of the enemy infantry. ∎

Above: French cavalry charges were launched in an attempt to decide the battle of Minden, but were thrown back by tenacious English defence and heavy musket fire.

Right: The map clearly shows the isolation of Sporcken's column.

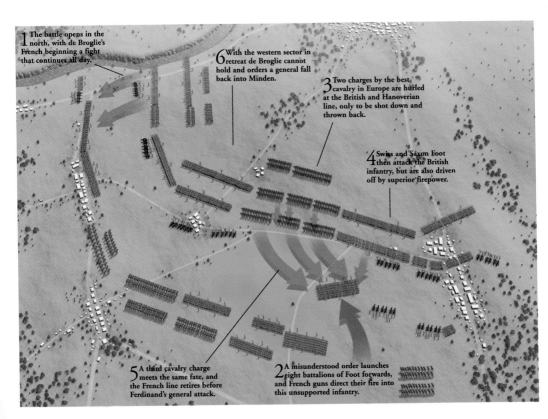

1 The battle opens in the north, with de Broglie's French beginning a fight that continues all day.

6 With the western sector in retreat de Broglie cannot hold and orders a general fall back into Minden.

3 Two charges by the best cavalry in Europe are hurled at the British and Hanoverian line, only to be shot down and thrown back.

4 Swiss and Saxon Foot then attack the British infantry, but are also driven off by superior firepower.

5 A third cavalry charge meets the same fate, and the French line retires before Ferdinand's general attack.

2 A misunderstood order launches eight battalions of Foot forwards, and French guns direct their fire into this unsupported infantry.

IMPERIAL DISASTERS
1760 – 1900

The eighteenth and nineteenth centuries produced military leaders of both shining brilliance and grievous incompetence. Sometimes the two poles met on the same battlefield – the tactical talent of Napoleon Bonaparte overwhelmed the muddle-headed General Mack at Ulm in 1805, with Mack surrendering 50,000 Austrian troops to Napoleon without a significant fight. Yet on other occasions a leader renowned for his victories suffered from personal campaign disasters. The hero of Waterloo, the Duke of Wellington, is less well known for his appalling handling of the month-long siege of Burgos in 1812, which cost the lives of 2000 of his soldiers for no physical gain whatsoever.

Left: Ambrose Burnside lost 12,000 troops at the bloody battle of Fredericksburg in 1862.

SARATOGA

THE BATTLE OF SARATOGA WAS A DEFINING MOMENT DURING THE AMERICAN WAR OF INDEPENDENCE (1775–85).

In 1777, following two years of inconclusive skirmishing and battles, the British were eager to lure the American forces out into a conclusive engagement. To this end, the flamboyant Major General John Burgoyne led a mixed British, German, Canadian and Indian force of some 7300 men down from Canada along the Hudson River. The purpose of the Canadian offensive was to cut off rebels in New England from southern support. Opposing Burgoyne would be around 12,000 American militia and regular Continental Army troops.

THE ATTACK STALLED

The advance down the Hudson proved to be a terrible ordeal for the British. Progress was painfully slow, hampered by the tactics of the American militia – paths blocked by fallen trees and accurate sniping, which killed many officers and men. Furthermore, supplies were running painfully short, and men began to go hungry. Nevertheless, there were British ➤➤

KEY FACTS

June 1777 – A British force of 7300 soldiers (later swelling to around 11,000) begins a southwards advance down the Hudson River against American rebel forces.

British forces are first stopped, then heavily defeated in two battles fought around present-day Saratoga on 19 September and 7 October.

The British survivors surrender on 17 October.

The British officer Major-General John Burgoyne surrenders his sword and his troops to General Horatio Gates. Burgoyne had spent a full week negotiating the terms of the surrender.

Above: A contemporary drawing of a captain in the American militia. The regional militias proved very effective combatants against the more formal British Army.

victories – Fort Ticonderoga fell on 1 July, and, on 19 September, the British attacked an American fortified camp at Bemis Heights (located in present-day Saratoga and Stillwater). American troops intercepted the British three-column advance around a clearing called Freeman Farm, and after a three-hour battle the Americans were defeated; however, Burgoyne was unable to prosecute the attack further.

DEFEAT AT FREEMAN FARM

Freeman Farm was around 1.6km (1 mile) north of the main American positions, and Burgoyne decided to camp there with his much-depleted force of around 4000 men. He waited for a British southern advance to reach him, but this did not come, and with supplies dwindling he went on the attack again on 7 October. Burgoyne was now facing around 12,000 troops and militia. In only one hour, the British lost 400 men to heavy American firepower and were eventually pushed into northward retreat and final surrender on 17 October 1777. The defeat at Saratoga was a tactical disaster for Burgoyne's force (only 1500 escaped capture), but also a strategic disaster for the British. It encouraged the French to join the war, which in turn sounded the death knell for British rule over America. ■

American infantry are formed into their ranks during the battle of Saratoga.

ULM

**THE CATASTROPHE WHICH OVERTOOK THE AUSTRIAN ARMY AT
ULM IN 1805 WAS A COMBINATION OF THE INEPTNESS OF ITS OWN
COMMANDER, GENERAL KARL FRIEHERR MACK VON LIEBERICH,
AND THE BRILLIANCE OF HIS OPPONENT, NAPOLEON BONAPARTE.**

Napoleon, his plans to invade England put on hold, turned
eastwards to face an Austro-Russian alliance. He realized that the
combined forces of his enemy would be too great in strength, so
he advanced his Grande Armeé at great speed towards the Rhine,
aiming to defeat the Austrians before the Russians could join
them. Mack completely failed to keep track of the French advance,
being a man more suited to methodical administration than swift
and tactical decision-making. On 16 October 1805, before he
knew it, his 80,000-strong army had been encircled at Ulm, about
77km (48 miles) southeast of Stuttgart.

INADEQUATE LEADERSHIP

Mack now had two basic options – to make a powerful defence
of the town's entry points, or to attempt a break-out across the
Danube and retreat into Austria. He followed the worst possible ➤➤

KEY FACTS

- **16 October 1805** – 80,000 Austrian troops under General Mack are surrounded at Ulm.
- **20 October** – Mack surrenders 50,000 of his soldiers to Napoleon without a significant fight.
- **13 November** – Napoleon takes Vienna.

Napoleon arranges his forces at Ulm. Ulm was one of Napoleon's most complete victories, as he defeated an 80,000-strong Austrian army at the cost only 6000 casualties. His success was compounded by the ineptitude of his Austrian opponents.

Above: Napoleon rides around the battlefield of Ulm, inspecting the aftermath. In a testimony to the close relationship between Napoleon and his troops, the commander had given his overcoat to a dying grenadier.

course – he did nothing. Mental paralysis seems to have overcome him, even as the French shelled the town.

MACK'S FAILURE

His second-in-command, Archduke Ferdinand, did attempt a break-out with a force of 25,000 men, and indeed came close to puncturing the French lines near Haslack. However, Mack inexplicably recalled Ferdinand's men, their sacrifice having been for nothing. Ferdinand subsequently attempted a unilateral break-out, but this was defeated with heavy casualties and the French surged forwards to take 26,000 prisoners. Mack could take no more, and on 20 October he surrendered 50,000 troops to the French, most of whom had not fired their weapons at all. Napoleon's forces had lost only 6000 men throughout the whole battle. Ulm saw Napoleon at his best, using speed and manoeuvre to outwit an enemy with slower decision-making processes. Yet the battle also saw the consequences of inept leadership. Had Mack thrown his full weight into a break-out, he may have been able to save an entire Austrian army, the loss of which permitted Napoleon to take Vienna without combat on 13 November. ∎

The Austrian commander, General Mack, is here seen surrendering his troops to Napoleon following his quite disastrous leadership at the battle of Ulm. He was subsequently court martialled for the surrender.

AUSTERLITZ

FOLLOWING THE DISASTER AT ULM (SEE PREVIOUS ENTRY), THE ALLIED ARMIES OF RUSSIA AND AUSTRIA SOUGHT TO REDRESS THE BALANCE AGAINST THE VICTORIOUS SOLDIERS OF NAPOLEON.

The French had already occupied Vienna, and Napoleon set off in pursuit of the Allies into Bavaria. His objective was to inflict a final crushing defeat before the Allies could catch breath, and also before his own soldiers ran out of energy. (In the march from northern France, Napoleon's Grande Armée had averaged around 23km/14 miles a day for five weeks).

LURED INTO A TRAP

The Allies turned to face Napoleon's 73,000 troops near Austerlitz in Moravia, deploying around 86,000 Austrian and Russian troops, the Russian general Kutuzov being in command. The Allies' plan was relatively simple: to attack and crush Napoleon's right flank, severing the French from the 22,000-strong garrison left in Vienna, while also rolling up the left flank and centre. This plan was encouraged by the fact that Napoleon seemed to have overextended his right flank, and had pulled his troops off the ➤➤

KEY FACTS

2 December 1805 – an Austro-Russian army of 86,000 troops battles with 73,000 French soldiers at Austerlitz.

The allies fall into Napoleon's trap, attacking his right flank with the mass of their forces and, by consequence, exposing themselves to flanking attack.

9.00 a.m. – Nicolas de Soult's IV Corps attacks the French centre, and the Allied left flank is cut off and as a consequence collapses.

A panoramic view of Austerlitz. The rugged nature of the terrain helped the French to mask their intentions, and so the Austro-Russian army thinned out its centre (the Pratzen Heights are visible bottom right) and exposed itself to a flanking attack.

Above: A long-range view of the battle of Austerlitz in progress. The key to victory in many nineteenth century battles was rapid command-and-control systems – the side that could move large formations more coherently and faster than the opponent usually won.

Pratzen Heights, which commanded the centre of the battlefield. At this stage, the Allies had no suspicion that they were falling into a devastating trap.

AUSTRO-RUSSIAN COLLAPSE

The battle of Austerlitz was fought on 2 December 1805, and began with a huge Allied thrust against the French right flank. French reinforcements stabilized the flank, much to the annoyance of the Allies, who pushed in more and more men, outnumbering the French there by four-to-one. Yet the Allied commanders could not see that their own left flank was becoming terribly exposed, and around 9.00 a.m. Napoleon unleashed Marshal Nicolas de Soult's IV Corps against Pratzen and the Allied centre. Kutozov committed his reserves, resulting in an epic cavalry battle, but Soult's forces were able to rout the Allied left flank. Allied resistance collapsed, and troops scattered in panic, some attempting to cross the frozen Satschen Lake to the south of the battlefield, where many fell through the ice. The Allied disaster was total. Austro-Russian forces had lost 26,000 men – dead or captured – against Napoleon's losses of 9000 soldiers. Austerlitz was confirmation of not only Napoleon's mastery of the battlefield, but also the unimaginative limits of Allied generalship. ∎

The figure of Napoleon dominates this image of the destruction on the battlefield at Austerlitz. Austerlitz was probably Napoleon's greatest battlefield victory, the emperor having defeated the combined might of Austrian and Russian armies.

JENA/AUERSTADT

THE BATTLE OF JENA/AUERSTADT IN 1806 DEMONSTRATED HOW DISASTROUSLY OUTDATED THE PRUSSIAN ARMY HAD BECOME.

Prussia declared war on Napoleonic France in August 1806, and by October had marshalled a Prussian-Saxon army of around 114,000 troops to take on the French.

WEAKENED BY DISAGREEMENT

Problems began immediately. The Prussian army was led by Charles William Ferdinand, Duke of Brunswick, but from the start there were major disagreements about strategy between himself and the Prussian general Prince Hohenlohe. Finally, it was agreed to advance the army towards Stuttgart and attempt to split the French forces and cut their lines of communication westwards; however, further command disagreements plagued the deployment. Unfortunately for the Prussians, Napoleon was already undoing their plans by marching his army through the Thuringerwald forest region, in an attempt to catch the Prussians in the flank or rear.

On 14 October, the date of the battle, the Prussian army was occupying two positions: about 63,000 men were at Auerstadt in Saxony, with another 51,000 troops set around 21km (13 miles) to the south ➤

KEY FACTS

14 October 1806 – A Prussian army of 114,000 men faces around 122,000 French troops around Jena/Auerstadt in Saxony.

The first battle at Jena results in a Prussian rout, then Napoleon unexpectedly encounters the bulk of the Prussian army at Auerstadt.

The Prussians at Auerstadt use piecemeal attacks, but cannot overcome a French defence and are defeated, with more than 40,000 men lost.

The French cavalry commander Marshal Joachim Murat leads his men towards victory at Jena. Murat had joined the cavalry at age 20 in 1787 and became a marshal in 1804 after a rapid rise up the officer ranks.

Above: Napoleon takes a ride around the town of Jena with his senior officers following his victory on the nearby battlefield. During his trip through the streets he met the legendary German philosopher Hegel.

around Jena. The Prussians at Jena were the first to be attacked, thrown on the defensive by around 54,000 of Napoleon's troops. The Prussians were outnumbered, outmanoeuvred and outgunned, and a terrible slaughter ensued. Hohenlohe attempted to form his troops up in defensive ranks around the village of Vierzenheiligen, but this simply allowed French artillery to blast into the close-packed ranks of 20,000 Prussian soldiers. By midday, the Prussians around Jena had been defeated.

OPPORTUNITY WASTED

Even so, there was an opportunity for Prussian salvation. At Auerstadt, two French corps were attempting to attack Hohenlohe from the rear, but unexpectedly encountered the bulk of the Prussian army there. The French initially fell back, giving their enemy an advantage, which the Prussians then threw away by making unsupported cavalry attacks against solid French squares. Unsurprisingly, these piecemeal assaults were unable to overcome the resolute French, then came news that Jena had fallen and that Brunswick had been killed. Demoralized, the Prussian army collapsed into defeat, its lines shot to pieces by artillery: it suffered 24,000 casualties, while 20,000 men fell prisoner. The defeat finally buried long-standing notions of the superiority of the Prussian military. ■

Napoleon and fellow officers reconnoiter the battleground at Jena in readiness for combat. Napoleon was a truly professional officer who dedicated himself totally to the study and practice of war.

RETREAT FROM MOSCOW

Napoleon's winter campaign into Russia in 1812 is the archetypal military disaster.

Some 600,000 French soldiers invaded Russia on 23 June 1812, yet only 20,000 survivors crossed back into Prussia in November of that same year.

Strategic retreat

Napoleon invaded Russia with the intention of drawing the Russian forces into a decisive battle and defeating them, then dictating the terms for peace. Aware that the advance of 800km (500 miles) to Moscow from the Duchy of Warsaw would be a formidable logistical challenge, he created an enormous supply train to follow his troops. Even so, he had underestimated his requirements. And once he had crossed into Russia, the Russians adopted a strategy of retreat-in-depth, pulling back rather than engaging in battle, and destroying any supplies or crops useful to the enemy, thus stretching the French supply system to breaking point.

That breaking point was soon reached. By the time Napoleon's army reached Smolensk in mid-August, it had lost at least 90,000 ➤➤

KEY FACTS

23 June 1812 – Napoleon invades Russia with 600,000 men.

Apart from a major engagement at Borodino on 7 September, the Russians retreat rather than fight, and the French army collapses through starvation and disease.

19 October – the French begin a retreat back from a deserted and incinerated Moscow, with only 20,000 men reaching final safety.

Although the French secured a major victory over the Russians at Borodino, every action inflicted losses on their ranks which they were steadily unable to sustain.

men through disease and starvation. Nevertheless, the Grande Armée remained a powerful foe. Russian and French forces finally clashed at Borodino on 7 September, a huge action that cost the French 30,000 casualties; the Russians 40,000. The victory was narrowly a French one, but still the Russians did not sue for peace, continuing instead to retreat. On 14 September, Napoleon took over a deserted Moscow, which Russian troops had set on fire to leave little shelter and almost no food there for the French. By 19 October, Napoleon's army had lost more than 500,000 men. With no sign of Russian capitulation, Napoleon was forced to order a retreat.

SLOW DEATH

The retreat from Moscow was a scarcely imaginable horror. Everything remotely edible was consumed, including crows, rats and the army's horses; cases of cannibalism were even recorded. The Russian winter froze thousands of men to death as they marched or slept, while constant attacks from Cossack Russians spread fear and death. The attempt to cross the frozen Berezina River itself cost 13,000 men their lives. Napoleon's disaster in Russia made a major contribution towards his abdication and exile to Elba in 1814, yet the irrepressible man would return the following year to bring war once again to Europe. ■

Above: The retreat from Moscow was a horrific episode in nineteenth-century military history. By only two weeks after leaving Moscow, 30,000 of the French army's horses had died, leaving soldiers to tramp through the winter snows on foot.

An eyewitness to the Moscow fire, Baron Meneval, described the conflagration as 'one mighty furnace from which sheaves of fire burst heavenwards, lighting up the horizon'.

BURGOS

THE DUKE OF WELLINGTON IS REGARDED AS ONE OF BRITAIN'S FINEST COMMANDERS, YET IN 1812, DURING THE PENINSULAR WAR (1808–14), HE CONDUCTED A SIEGE OPERATION OF BREATHTAKING INCOMPETENCE, COSTING THE LIVES OF 2000 MEN.

In September 1812, Wellington was tasked with taking the walled fortress city of Burgos in Castile, which was occupied by around 2000 well-armed French troops under the professional leader General Dubreton. Wellington treated his objective casually, taking only a few thousand British and Portuguese infantry, 13 engineers or sappers and only eight 24-pound cannon – amazingly, he turned down an offer of more heavy cannon from Admiral Home Popham, a decision he would bitterly regret.

UNDERMINED BY INCOMPETENCE

Wellington's first action at Burgos was an infantry attack launched against a peripheral defensive position called the Hornwork. Wellington took the position, but his unit incurred 421 casualties, while the assault against the walls of the Burgos fortification itself cost another 200 casualties and still allowed Burgos to remain ➤➤

KEY FACTS

September 1812 – Wellington lays siege to the French-occupied fortress of Burgos with a mixed British and Portuguese infantry force and inadequate engineering and siege resources.

Wellingtons's force is unable to take Burgos, whether through infantry assault, artillery barrages or mining.

22 October – Wellington calls off the siege, having lost 2000 men in two months.

The French soldiers in Burgos withstood every British attempt to break into its fortifications. However, in 1813, another attempt to take Burgos was far more successful, the French-occupied fortress falling in only two days.

Above: Arthur Wellesley, the Duke of Wellington, was generally a careful military commander who attempted to reduce the number of battle casualties.

unbreached. Wellington then tried to breach the fortress through explosive power. First he used a 454kg (1000lb) mine, which was intended to destroy the northwest wall of the fort, but an error in underground navigation meant that the explosion simply destroyed the walls of a nearby medieval castle instead. A feeble artillery bombardment from Wellington's eight cannon was equally ineffectual, and indeed invited an artillery response from the French, which destroyed most of the British batteries. Although a subsequent British mine did make a minor breach in the French walls, the following infantry attack was repelled, at a cost of 220 British casualties.

COUNTERATTACKS

Seeing the incompetence of their foe, the French grew bolder, and even sent out their own successful raiding parties against the British trenches and positions. Finally, on 22 October, Wellington admitted that Burgos would not be taken and the siege was lifted. A total of 2000 British or Portuguese soldiers had been killed, mainly through the fault of command, while Dubreton lost around 300 troops. Thankfully for Wellington, his disaster at Burgos would be overshadowed by later victories. ∎

Wellington's infantry are here seen preparing to deliver volley fire during an action in the Peninsular War. The necessity of effective musket volleys explains much of the formation tactics of nineteenth century warfare.

AFGHANISTAN

Few military disasters in British imperial military history are equal to that which occurred in 1842 in Afghanistan.

In 1838, British forces entered Afghanistan and, aided by bullet and cannon, installed the puppet ruler Shah Shuja. Afghanistan was largely a wild, tribal and lawless country, and the British occupiers faced a constant guerrilla war.

Continual attacks

In 1841, however, the sporadic fighting coalesced into an organized general revolt, which sought to eject the British from Afghanistan. Around Kabul at this time was a large force of 4500 soldiers (mixed European and colonial) and 12,000 civilian camp followers under the control of the elderly, sickly and indecisive Major General William Elphinstone, who had been unwillingly clawed out of half-pay retirement by Lord Auckland, the governor general of India. With rebellious Afghan tribes now on every side of the city, the British were in a perilous position. They were located just outside the city in sprawling cantonments which were almost impossible to defend adequately, thanks to the previous commander, Major General Sir Willoughby Cotton. The British found themselves under siege from 2 November, but on New Year's Day negotiations resulted ➤➤

KEY FACTS

November 1841 – general Afghan revolt against the British-installed government of Shah Shuja and the British forces in Afghanistan.

6 January 1842 – British column of 4500 soldiers and 12,000 camp followers set out from Kabul to march to Jelalabad, a distance of about 130km (80 miles).

Over the next two weeks, the column is destroyed by Afghan raids, only one Briton reaching safety at Jelalabad.

Afghanistan was a troubled region for the British throughout the reign of Queen Victoria. Its fragmented tribal structures made British governance almost impossible, while its mountainous landscape was ideal for guerrilla war.

Above: The British passage through the Khurd-Kabul pass saw 3000 people killed. The Afghan warriors had startling talent in long-range sniping using extended barrel muskets.

in the British committing themselves to marching out of Kabul to Jelalabad 130km (80 miles) away. The march would be made with all 16,500 people, through the Afghan mountain passes, in the heart of winter, and via the territories of numerous hostile Afghan tribes (a promised escort by Akhbar, son of deposed Afghan leader Dost Muhammed, did not materialize).

MURDEROUS ATTACKS

The British column set out from Kabul on 6 January 1842, and within only a few miles of the cantonments Afghan warriors began raiding attacks, picking off stragglers, killing with long-range musket fire and slaughtering rearguard troops. After two days of retreating, the column had lost hundreds of people for an advance of only 16km (10 miles). Worse was to come. The Khurd-Kabul pass was narrow and 8km (5 miles) long, and the journey through it resulted in 3000 deaths from Afghan blades and rifle fire. By the end of the fifth day, only 450 soldiers and 3000 camp followers remained upright, almost all suffering from hunger and frostbite. Finally, on 13 January, a single rider – Surgeon William Brydon – made it to the safety of the British fort at Jelalabad. He was the only Briton to make it; apart from a handful of stragglers, the rest of the column had been slaughtered, with a few taken captive. ■

Dr William Brydon, assistant surgeon in the Bengal Army and the sole survivor of the journey from Kabul, arrives at the gates of Jelalabad with his horse dying beneath him.

ANTIETAM

IT IS HARD TO DETERMINE EXACTLY WHOSE DISASTER IT WAS AT THE BATTLE OF ANTIETAM (ALSO KNOWN AS THE BATTLE OF SHARPSBURG).

The fight between General George B. McClellan, leading the Union Army of the Potomac, and Confederate general Robert E. Lee, leading the Army of Northern Virginia, was a failure for both sides, but particularly for McClellan. And it was the single bloodiest day of the Civil War.

FAILURE OF NERVE
The lead-up to the battle began on 4 September 1862, when Lee crossed the Potomac River to invade Maryland. The subsequent week saw each side fighting for advantage, but by 14 September the two armies were concentrated around the town of Sharpsburg, west of Antietam Creek. McClellan, an unusually cautious leader, was feeling confident about overcoming his enemy, as a copy of the entire Confederate battleplan had fallen into his possession some days earlier. Furthermore, he outnumbered the Confederates nearly two-to-one (75,000 men to 40,000 men).

The battle of Antietam began on the morning of 17 September, the first move coming from the Union right flank, which threw itself in repeated and uncoordinated assaults across a cornfield against ➤➤

> **KEY FACTS**
>
> **Battle fought** on 17 September 1862 between Union forces under McClellan and Confederate forces under Lee.
>
> **Battle degenerates** into an appalling slaughter, with McClellan in particular missing numerous opportunities to decide the battle by committing his reserve forces.
>
> **Combined death** toll of 25,700.

The Rohrbach Bridge, also known as Burnside's Bridge, which straddled Antietam Creek, was the site of some of the bloodiest fighting during the Antietam battle. The rifles of 400 Georgian infantry were concentrated onto the bridge.

a Confederate Corps led by 'Stonewall' Jackson. All the attacks were repelled, but at the cost of 10,000 casualties, with the cornfield changing hands on 15 occasions.

SENSELESS WASTE

Union troops did achieve a breakthrough in the Confederate centre, but now McClellan's caution kicked in and he held back the reserve of 20,000 men, thus allowing the Confederates to restore the line. More critically, the Union general Ambrose Burnside attacked the enemy's right flank by leading it persistently over the narrow Rohrbach Bridge, despite the fact that the Antietam was easily forded. This led to enormous casualties, but eventually the Confederate right was pushed back to Sharpsburg. McClellan, however, again failed to commit his reserve to secure the battle. Confederate reinforcements then arrived, and Burnside retreated. The battle now petered out, both sides sickened by the horrific slaughter. Lee's troops retreated, unthreatened by McClellan, who was subsequently dismissed from his post. Left behind on the battlefield were the bodies of some 12,000 Union troops and 13,700 Confederate men, their lives lost to incompetent and overcautious leadership. ∎

Above: President Abraham Lincoln, here seen in his classic garb in the centre, visited the Union camp after the battle of Antietam. The two men on his flanks are Major Allan Pinkerton (left) and General McClellan.

A view of the Union signal tower at Elk Mountain, which overlooked the Antietam battlefield.

FREDERICKSBURG

FREDERICKSBURG WAS THE FIRST BATTLE OF THE UNION ARMY OF THE POTOMAC UNDER ITS NEW COMMANDER, AMBROSE BURNSIDE, WHO HAD TAKEN THE POSITION AFTER PRESIDENT LINCOLN DISMISSED THE POPULAR GENERAL MCCLELLAN FROM THE POST.

Burnside guided a Union advance into Virginia on 26 October 1862, then attempted to make an outflanking manoeuvre against General Robert E. Lee's forces by crossing the Rappahannock River near Fredericksburg.

AN EXERCISE IN FUTILITY

However, three weeks passed before adequate pontoon bridges arrived, and Lee was able to adopt strong defensive positions around Fredericksburg from 20 November, utilizing a ridgeline set back from the Rappahannock. Even after Burnside's bridges arrived on 25 November, he seemed in no rush to go on the offensive, despite the fact that the Confederate general Jackson was heading to Fredericksburg with reinforcements.

In early December, Burnside finally decided that the time was right for battle to begin. His battleplan was to cross the river, ➤➤

KEY FACTS

- **26 October 1862** – a Union army under Burnside moves into Virginia and faces Confederate forces around Fredericksburg.
- **Burnside allows** a three-week delay in crossing the Rappahannock River, giving the Confederates time to prepare defences.
- **13 December 1862** – Burnside throws his men away in fruitless attacks against Confederate troops, resulting in 12,000 dead.

Burnside's Union troops make a bloody attempt to cross the Rappahannock River, against Confederate troops occupying excellent defensive positions. Note the pontoon bridge being constructed in the bottom right of the picture.

advance to take a road just behind the Confederate lines, then branch out left and right along the road in envelopment attacks. It was a high-risk operation, but the first pontoon bridges were laid on the water on 11 December.

RIVER CROSSING

For the next two days, Burnside's infantry put down more bridges, all the while taking heavy casualties from Confederate marksmen on the other side of the river. Finally, on 13 December, Burnside ordered the infantry to attack. The next few hours would have been farcical were they not so horrific. The Union troops on the right flank made nine separate assaults against a stone-wall defence on Marye's Heights, taking thousands of casualties without any tactical progress. On the left flank, the Grand Division did penetrate the enemy line in one place, but Burnside gave them no follow-up support and they were eventually forced to retreat, having lost nearly 50 per cent of their strength.

By the end of the day, the Union assaults were called off, effectively ending the battle of Fredericksburg. For Burnside, it had been a bloody exercise in futility – 12,000 Union dead against just 5000 Confederate dead. ■

Ambrose Burnside was born in 1824. He graduated from West Point in 1847, but his service during the American Civil War was erratic, and he resigned from the army in 1865.

Union troops attempt to take the Confederate heights at Fredericksburg. The American Civil War saw new rifle technologies reach the battlefield, including breech-loading cartridge weapons, and these added to the high death toll of Civil War battles.

LITTLE BIGHORN

THE BATTLE OF LITTLE BIGHORN WAS A DISASTER CAUSED BY THE IMPETUOUS LEADERSHIP OF THE INFAMOUS LIEUTENANT-COLONEL GEORGE ARMSTRONG CUSTER.

On June 1876, during the Indian Wars, a large force of US infantry and cavalry gathered in southeastern Montana.

A RASH DECISION

Their purpose was to displace a significant movement of Lakota and Cheyenne Indians and drive them back into reservations in Dakota Territory. The American troops had manoeuvred together in three columns, one of them led by General Alfred Terry. Part of Terry's command was a force of US 7th Cavalry troops under Custer, and on 22 June they were sent out by Terry from positions near the Yellowstone River. Custer's force numbered just over 600 when, on 25 June, Crow Indian scouts working with the cavalry reported a large Indian encampment in the valley of Little Bighorn, about 24km (15 miles) to the west.

The cautious action would have been to wait to link up with the main body of Terry's infantry before acting, as the number of Indian warriors present in the encampment was not known. ➤➤

KEY FACTS

25 June 1876 – Troops of the US 7th cavalry led by Custer spot a large encampment of Sioux and Cheyenne Indians around Little Bighorn.

Custer attacks the Sioux-Cheyenne encampment, but his troops are soon overwhelmed by 2000 counterattacking Indians.

Two of Custer's three battalion columns are forced into retreat with heavy casualties, while Custer's column, about 210 strong, is massacred to the last man.

Custer's men fight to the death around Little Bighorn, attempting to postpone a terrible end.

Above: The ill-fated General Custer, here seen striking a portrait pose in the classic garments of a frontiersman.

Instead, Custer, fearing that the Indians would slip away, divided his force up into three battle commands – Major Reno's command was directed to attack from the south, while Custer's command of 210 men would move into the hills to the north and attack from the encampment from there. A third command under Major Benteen would circle out to the southwest.

FIGHT TO THE DEATH

Only when Reno mounted his attack did the strength of the Indian encampment become apparent, there being some 2000 Lakota and Cheyenne warriors there. Although initially surprised, the Indians quickly counterattacked, and Reno soon found himself having to adopt defensive positions, surrounded by mounted Indians and warriors on foot. As casualties started to mount, Reno ordered the survivors, along with Benteen's men, who had now joined them, to retreat into nearby wooded hills, where they would fight for survival for the next two days. Custer's command, meanwhile, had been surrounded about 6.4km (4 miles) away on hilly ground. Few facts are really known of how they died, except that every soldier – including Custer himself – was slaughtered, their naked and mutilated bodies being discovered scattered around Little Big Horn, most on what is today known, appropriately, as Last Stand Hill. ∎

Memorials are erected to the men of the US 7th Cavalry killed at Little Bighorn. In 1879 the battlefield was designated a national cemetery, the keeping of the site entrusted to the War Department.

ISANDHLWANA

A COMMON INGREDIENT IN MANY OF THE DISASTERS THAT BEFELL THE BRITISH ARMY DURING THE VICTORIAN PERIOD WAS A CHRONIC UNDERESTIMATION OF THE ENEMY.

Such was indeed the case when 17,000 British and Allied native troops invaded Zululand in January 1879.

INSUFFICIENT PREPARATION

The invasion was engineered by the South African governor general Sir Henry Bartle Edward Frere, and was part of the British plan to colonize (or 'Confederate') all of southern Africa under British rule. The troops were led by Lieutenant General Frederic Theisger, Lord Chelmsford from October that year. Chelmsford crossed Zululand in January 1879, following a collapse in what was a British pretence at diplomacy. His troops deployed in three columns. The central column, which included Chelmsford himself, advanced to make camp on the plain around Isandhlwana hill, about 16km (10 miles) from the British crossing point of Rourke's Drift on the Buffalo River.

Chelmsford's column was about 2800 strong, and such was his confidence that he did not make any physical defensive arrangements around the camp, but simply posted out pickets in the surrounding hills. On 20 January, Chelmsford began to send out large scouting parties in search of the Zulu army, ➤➤

KEY FACTS

11 January 1878 – British forces deploy into Zululand. Large column under Lord Chelmsford camps around Isandhlwana.

Chelmsford does not make adequate defensive arrangements for the camp, and almost halves its strength by taking out scouting units.

22,000 Zulus attack the camp on 22 January, killing over 1300 British and Allied troops.

The valiant British square resists Zulu attacks. The British soldier in the Zulu Wars were armed with the Martini-Henry rifle, a weapon firing an enormous .45-calibre round, which frequently passed through several Zulus on its killing trajectory.

leaving only about 1700 troops at Isandhlwana. Some Royal Engineers arrived to reinforce on the 22nd, but their commanding officer, Colonel Anthony Durnford, took over the camp and himself sent out recce groups, further weakening the camp's defence. Scouting parties had already made contact with some Zulu warriors, but later on the 22nd, the British at Isandhlwana suddenly found themselves attacked by over 20,000 Zulu warriors.

OVERWHELMED

The Zulus, contrary to British judgements, were actually a sophisticated warrior society, arranged in *impi* (regimental-type formations) and well led by warrior-officers. The initial ranks of spear-armed Zulus were inevitably torn open by British rifle fire, but inadequate resupply arrangements meant that the British were soon running out of firepower. They were engulfed, and only 55 Europeans and around 300 native troops survived the resulting massacre in the camp. Chelmsford had not given reports of the battle due attention, and only at night, when his units returned to Isandhlwana, did he realize the strength of the enemy. The dead were scattered around the camp, all of the corpses having been disembowelled, a traditional Zulu practice. ∎

The British at Isandhlwana were simply overwhelmed by sheer weight of Zulu numbers. The Zulu dead left on the battlefield heavily outnumbered those suffered by the British.

Although the British soldiers would have opened volley fire at around 350m (1148ft), the battle was soon at close quarters.

ADOWA

ITALY BEGIN ITS COLONIAL INTRUSIONS INTO ETHIOPIA IN 1885, THE RESULT BEING A SERIES OF SMALL, BLOODY CONFLICTS THAT USUALLY, THOUGH NOT ALWAYS, SAW THE ITALIANS EMERGE AS VICTORS OVER THE RUDIMENTARY TACTICS AND WEAPONS OF THE ETHIOPIANS.

However, by the end of 1889, a new and judicious king, Menelik II, revolutionized Ethiopian military affairs by heavy investment in magazine-loaded rifles and modern artillery.

BREAKING THE STALEMATE

Having previously enjoyed generally good relations with the Italians, Menelik signed the Treaty of Wichale on 2 May 1889. He was under the impression that the treaty gave him sovereignty while ceding certain northern regions to the Italians. However, the Italian-language version of the treaty effectively committed him to surrendering that sovereignty.

As a result, in February 1893, when he realized that he had been double-crossed, Menelik rejected the treaty. In response, Italy decided to take over Ethiopia as a protectorate. The governor of Eritrea, General Oreste Baratieri, secured some rapid victories with his professional army of around 25,000

Colonial dominance in African became problematic for many European nations in the late 1800s with the increasing use of modern firearms by African tribes, as was proved at Adowa.

Menelik II became the emperor of Ethiopia in 1889, and successfully united the Ethiopian tribes in resistance to Italian attempts to turn Ethiopia into an Italian protectorate. After the Italian defeat at Adowa, Ethiopia was recognized as a sovereign state.

men, many of whom were indigenous Askari troops. However, Ethiopian victories at Amba Alagi and Makalle in 1895 forced the two sides to stalemate, Menelik taking up position at Adowa and Baratieri at Adigrat, then Sauria.

DEVASTATING ATTACK

On 25 February 1896, the Italian premier Francesco Crispi ordered Baratieri to attack. (Ironically, just a few more weeks of waiting would probably have forced Menelik to disband his army.) On the night of 29 February, Baratieri advanced 17,700 troops and 56 guns from Sauria in four brigades. However, the precipitous and rocky terrain soon fragmented the march (a problem compounded by poor maps), with brigades merging, separating and becoming strung out. Furthermore, spies had alerted Menelik to the Italian approach, and around 100,000 troops swarmed out to meet them on the morning of 1 March. The Ethiopians fell upon the Italians in constant waves, supported by cannon positioned on high ground. Entire brigades were cut off and massacred, and by the end of the day the Italians had been forced to retreat, the force having lost nearly 50 per cent of its manpower. Although Ethiopia suffered 17,000 casualties (including 7000 dead), the Italian disaster around Adowa secured the Ethiopians sovereignty. ■

The Ethiopian army was, in 1889, one of the most advanced indigenous military forces on the African continent. Under its ruler, Menelik II, it had secured the purchase of 38,000 magazine-loading rifles and even of 28 pieces of field artillery. The army had only basic tactical control, however, which accounts for the appalling Ethiopian casualties (7000 dead) at Adowa.

SPION KOP

IN NOVEMBER 1899, WITH THE BOER WAR ONLY ONE MONTH OLD, THE BOERS LAID SIEGE TO THE TOWN OF LADYSMITH IN NORTHERN NATAL (A BRITISH COLONY).

The relief of Ladysmith became an overriding British objective, but first the British troops had to take an area of ridges and hills on the approaches to Ladysmith, with Spion Kop being the dominant feature.

BUNGLED OPPORTUNITIES

In mid-January 1900, a large British relief column of around 15,000 men, commanded by the elderly and incompetent Lieutenant General Sir Charles Warren, was tasked with securing the heights. So it was that on the night of 23 January a force of 1700 British soldiers, led by Major-General Edward Woodgate, ascended the southwestern slope of Spion Kop. At around 0400, the British reached the flat plateau summit in dense fog, which reduced visibility to less than 100m (328ft). They found and overcame a light Boer force of around 70 soldiers, suffering only three casualties. The mission seemed an early success, and the British ➤➤

The disaster at Spion Kop sent shock waves through British society, throwing up significant questions about the quality of military leadership within the British Army and marking further testament to the fighting capabilities of the Boers.

The British had been unable to dig proper trenches on Spion Kop. The ground was almost solid rock, and after some three hours of digging the trenches were only around 46cm (18in) deep.

spent the remainder of the night digging ineffectual trenches. When the sun rose and burnt away the fog, however, it transpired that there was another crest line further out and three other high points. All of these were occupied by the Boers, and they provided ideal positions from which to sweep the plateau with gunfire.

KILLING ZONE

Boer firepower subsequently wrought a fearful slaughter on the British troops packed into the 1.2 ha (3 acre) site, who were unable to dig in because of the rocky terrain (bodies were piled up as improvised defensive works). The Boer infantry reoccupied the British crest line after bloody close-quarter battle, and the British troops, many wounded, were low on ammunition and parched with thirst. Relief units were sent for, but bungling leadership prevented them for taking opportunities to defeat the Boers in flanking manoeuvres. Despite this, the British still held the plateau at 1800, but, without any clear leadership from Warren, orders were given for withdrawal from Spion Kop. When the Boers reoccupied the heights, they found 650 British dead; a further 554 were wounded and 170 taken prisoner. After the battle, there was a political explosion back in England as the protagonists sought to place the blame. It had been a shamefully costly example of military amateurism. ■

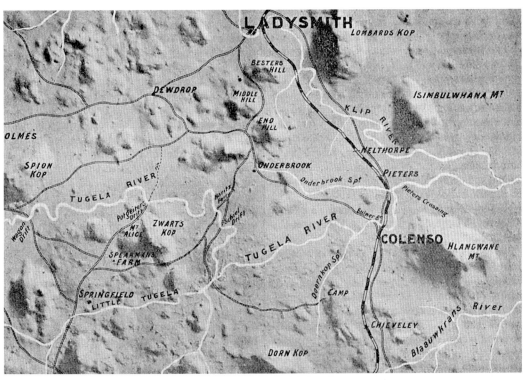

Spion Kop (left) is seen here in relation to the town of Ladysmith, the object of so much British bloodshed.

MODERN CATASTROPHES
1900 – PRESENT DAY

The military disasters of the twentieth century took on a scale unmatched by history. The world was convulsed by two world wars, the second of these costing an estimated 56 million lives, with half of this total being suffered by the Soviet Union alone. Individual battles during this war produced unprecedented death tolls – Stalingrad alone took one million lives. Although a tragedy on the scale of World War II has thankfully not been seen since 1945, the scattered conflicts of the Cold War and decolonization, plus counterterrorist operations, continued the catalogue of military disaster, from the rout of UN forces in Korea in 1950 to US mission failure on the streets of Mogadishu in 1993.

Left: The USA gained control of the Pacific at the battle of Midway in 1942.

GALLIPOLI

THE GALLIPOLI CAMPAIGN WAS A PRODIGIOUS FAILURE ON THE PART OF BRITISH AND COLONIAL FORCES TO OPEN A NEW FRONT IN THE MEDITERRANEAN DURING WORLD WAR I.

Gallipoli was a British response to a Russian request for a new front to be opened in the Mediterranean against Turkey, which had entered the war on the Germany's side in late 1914. Field Marshal Lord Kitchener, the Secretary of State for War, responded with a plan to take the Dardanelles, a thin strip of water between the Gallipoli peninsula and Turkey. This would provide access to the Sea of Marmara and a supply line to Russia.

NAVAL FAILURE

The first attempt to secure the Dardanelles was launched in February 1915, a purely naval operation that, despite some initial successes, resulted in the loss of two British and one French battleships on sea mines.

The British high command now opted for a land campaign to take Gallipoli. An initial amphibious landing was aborted owing to landing errors, which allowed the Turkish defenders time to ➤➤

KEY FACTS

February 1915 – A British attempt to take the Dardenelles eventually fails.

25 April 1915 – the Allies begin a land campaign to take the Gallipoli peninsula.

The Allied campaign becomes bogged down in a pointless war of attrition costing 205,000 casualties. The campaign is abandoned in late 1915.

A Turkish artillery shell explodes around Allied coastal positions on the Gallipoli peninsula.

reinforce before the actual landings took place on 25 April 1915. Proficient feints meant that the British were able to establish beachheads at Cape Helles at the south of the peninsula, while Australian and New Zealander troops occupied 'Anzac Cove' some 16km (10 miles) further up the eastern coastline.

EMERGING DISASTER

The Allies failed to exploit their grip on the peninsula successfully, and the British and Commonwealth troops were trapped under the Turkish guns and waves of disease. On 6–7 August – by which time the Allies had suffered around 30,000 casualties – the British made further landings at Suvla Bay, just to the north of Anzac Cove, in an attempt to break the deadlock. Through poor command and lack of initiative, all the landings achieved was to create more targets for the Turks.

Above: British soldiers evacuate the wounded from Gallipoli. During the campaign there was a terribly high attrition rate among Allied officers and NCOs, the Turks having fielded thousands of talented snipers trained to target the Allied leadership.

The battle dragged until Kitchener decided that the Allies should be evacuated from Gallipoli, a feat achieved by 9 January 1916. The Gallipoli campaign had cost the Allies 46,000 dead and more than 150,000 wounded.

Positions on the Allied beachheads around Gallipoli were chaotic, insanitary and exposed to constant Turkish shellfire.

VERDUN

THE BATTLE OF VERDUN WAS NOT A CLEAR-CUT DISASTER FOR EITHER THE GERMANS OR THE FRENCH, ALTHOUGH THE GERMANS DID FAIL IN THEIR OBJECTIVES OF TAKING THE TOWN AND ITS SURROUNDING FORTIFICATIONS.

It was, however, a disaster in brute terms of casualties, costing the lives of hundreds of thousands of men for no significant gain.

BATTLE OF ATTRITION

In December 1915, the German chief of staff, Erich von Falkenhayn, made recommendations to Kaiser Wilhelm II for winning the war. He not only proposed unrestricted submarine warfare in the Atlantic, but also outlined a massive offensive against the fortifications ringing the town of Verdun, which stood as a salient projecting out into the German lines. Falkenhayn's was an attritional plan – to draw the bulk of the French Army into the defence of Verdun, where, as he put it, he could 'bleed them white'. In the end, it was both sides who were drained of blood.

The German offensive began on 21 February 1916 with a huge 21-hour artillery bombardment, which concentrated 100,000 ➤➤

French infantry soldiers cower under the force of a German artillery barrage. As the ground became churned to mud, an increasingly high percentage of shells did not detonate, creating an unexploded ordnance problem for later generations.

Above: A French cartoon vividly evokes the spirit of French resistance at Verdun. The caption to the cartoon read 'The Germans won't be able to claim this as a victory.' Ultimately, the sheer scale of losses during the campaign question the French claim to have 'won' the battle.

shells every hour into Verdun's front, which was 13km (8 miles) long. Artillery was the defining weapon of Verdun, which was to be a battle of meat-grinders. The following infantry assault was made by the German Fifth Army, and it made initial good progress both sides of the river Meuse (the battlefield was bisected by the river).

AWESOME CASUALTIES

On the 25th, the powerful fort at Douament was taken. By this point, the French commander in chief, Joffre, had ordered all possible resources to Verdun, pouring reinforcements and supplies into the area down a single road that became known as the 'Voie Sacrée' (Sacred Road). The battle was costing enormous amounts of manpower, but dragged on into early July, with the Germans inching closer to Verdun itself. However, the British offensive at the Somme on 1 July relieved some pressure and allowed the French to go on the offensive. In December, by which time the French had retaken Douament and Fort Vaux, Hindeburg called off the offensive. Verdun was a true humanitarian disaster – 550,000 Germans and 434,000 French casualties were sustained, with 50 per cent fatalities. Perhaps even more so than the Somme, it symbolizes the sheer waste of World War I. ■

The French reinforcements pouring down the Voie Sacrée to Verdun faced a bleak future. In the week beginning 28 February alone, more than 190,000 soldiers travelled down the road to the front.

SOMME

THE BATTLE OF THE SOMME IN 1916 IS POPULARLY REGARDED AS THE ARCHETYPAL MILITARY DISASTER.

Field Marshal Douglas Haig's Somme offensive consisted of a push by three British armies and one French army on a front 50km (31 miles) long, the primary objectives for Day One being to take the German firstline trenches and the Pozières ridge, then to advance out to take Bapaume. The offensive began on 24 June with a six-day artillery barrage that fired 1.7 million shells into the German positions. However, around one third of the shells did not explode, and the German barbed-wire defences were rearranged, but generally uncut. German casualties were also reduced by their skill in underground bunker construction.

DEATH ON AN UNPRECEDENTED SCALE

The foot offensive, scheduled for 29 June, was delayed by two days owing to torrential downpours over the battlefield, which turned the landscape into sucking mud. However, British soldiers went over the top on 1 July and suffered a massacre unprecedented in British Army history. German machine-gun, small-arms and ➤➤

British troops occupy positions on the Western Front. Although most are armed with 7.7mm (.303in) Lee-Enfield rifles, the man in the foreground has a Lewis gun, an excellent weapon that pioneered the concept of the light machine gun.

artillery fire killed more than 20,000 soldiers in the first day alone, and wounded a further 36,000. Entire battalions were slashed down to a few hundred men.

MASSIVE CASUALTIES

The opening day of the Somme offensive was, however, just the first day of an offensive that continued until November. Casualties after 1 July dropped to an average of around 3000 per day (the total British casualties were 415,000), although there were occasional examples of much larger slaughter. French forces also suffered 200,000 casualties during the campaign. The German Army in the sector sustained 650,000 casualties, and the Somme offensive undoubtedly put a huge dent into German manpower and military capability. So perhaps the real disaster of the Somme was that its territorial gains were so slight – around only 10km (6 miles) at their deepest point, with some units taking until November to secure their objectives for Day One. The British Army, and British society in general, had made a colossal sacrifice for relatively insignificant gain. ■

Above: British mines are exploded under German lines at the opening of the Somme offensive. Ten mines were detonated on the first day of the battle, the largest of these contained 24 tons of ammonal explosive. The mines created defensive positions for British troops.

A medical aid station sits amid the blasted landscape of the Somme. In July 1916, two Victoria Crosses were awarded to stretcher bearers for their bravery in collecting wounded while under German fire.

DUNKIRK AND THE FALL OF FRANCE

As Winston Churchill said at the time, the miraculous escape of the British Army from Dunkirk should not blind us to the fact that it was a military disaster.

Viewed in its context – the fall of France – Dunkirk exemplifies the total bewilderment of Allied resistance against a daring and professional German blitzkrieg.

No defences

Germany's offensive plan against the Low Countries and France was conceived mainly by General von Manstein, and was simple and brilliant. An invasion of the Netherlands and Belgium by Army Group B would draw the bulk of the French army northwards, along with the 10 divisions of the British Expeditionary Force (BEF), while in the far south Army Group C would occupy the defenders of the French Maginot line. Between the two armies, Army Group A would drive through the Ardennes forest – which was undefended by the French, who considered it impassable – then cross the river Meuse around Sedan and drive through to the French coast. Launched on 10 May 1940, the German offensive ➤➤

KEY FACTS

10 May 1940 – The German offensive against France and the Low Countries begins.

French and British forces are committed to tackling German advances in the Netherlands and Belgium, allowing a surprise German attack through the Ardennes forest to drive into northern France and head for the English Channel.

The French and British are unable to respond. The BEF evacuates through Dunkirk and France capitulates on 22 June.

The German offensive in France entirely vindicated the concept of blitzkrieg. Wehrmacht infantry such as these would advance in the wake of mechanized, armoured units and utilized close air support in an entirely modern manner.

Above: France burns during the German advance of 1940. French forces were totally outclassed tactically and tried to re-fight the First World War.

began the collapse of western Europe. The Netherlands fell in four days, and three French armies and the BEF pushed northwards into the trap. Disastrously, the French retained no mobile reserve, so were left with limited options when the Panzers of Army Group A, which had advanced unhindered through the Ardennes, began pushing across the Meuse on 14 May.

ALLIED COLLAPSE

On almost every front, the Allies were routed, and poor deployment of French resources by General Gamelin allowed the Germans to reach the Channel by 20 May, despite having a vulnerable flank. With the British and French now trapped, the British evacuated from Dunkirk. Between 26 May and 2 June, more than 338,000 British and 120,000 French were evacuated. This was certainly a success, but it was paid for with the blood of many French and Belgian rearguard troops, and signalled that France was alone in its fate. (Belgium had surrendered on 28 May.) On 14 June, Paris fell; on 22 June, French leaders were forced to sign an armistice in the same railway carriage in which the Germans had signed their surrender in 1918. In a little over one month's fighting, the 144 divisions of troops from France, Belgium, the Netherlands and Britain had been routed by 141 divisions of German troops. ∎

Dunkirk was a huge victory for the Germans, despite the fact that so many British servicemen escaped to their homeland. The British were completely unprepared for the professionalism of the German campaign.

KIEV

SOVIET FORCES HAD BEEN IN A PARLOUS STATE FOLLOWING THE LAUNCH OF OPERATION BARBAROSSA, THE GERMAN INVASION OF THE SOVIET UNION, ON 22 JUNE 1941.

Operation Barbarossa was a huge three-pronged attack. Army Group North swung up towards Leningrad, Army Group Centre drove directly east towards Moscow, while Army Group South punched downwards towards Kiev and into the Ukraine.

TRAPPED BY STALIN'S ORDERS

It was Army Group South which faced the toughest onslaught, its progress delayed by tenacious counterattacks from the Soviet Fifth Army. However, it had reached to within 16km (10 miles) of Kiev by 11 July. On 29 July, Hitler made one of the most controversial decisions of the war. He ordered that Army Group Centre, after it had captured Smolensk, should stop its advance and send its Second Army and Second *Panzergruppe* south to assist the Ukrainian advance, with the primary aim being to encircle and destroy the forces of the Soviet Southwest Front around Kiev. Guderian's Panzers began their advance southwards on 25 August. ➤➤

German troops plan offensive manoeuvres in Russia. One of the reasons for the great German successes in Operation Barbarossa was that units down to platoon level were trained to show individual initiative in battle, unlike their Russian opponents.

The city of Kiev lies in ruins following heavy fighting. Some 15–20 million Soviet civilians would die in World War II, trapped between the warring armies.

Stalin still had time to pull his forces back before the jaws of the pincers snapped shut. However, Stalin refused to allow retreat – indeed, he sent in two more armies to reinforce the Kiev area. A counterattack by the Soviets around Gomel, north of Kiev, did not prevent General Kleist's First Panzer Group and Guderian's Second Panzer Group meeting on 16 September, 200km (124 miles) east of Kiev at Romny.

ENCIRCLEMENT

Any attempt at breakout was quashed by Stalin's orders, and the fate of the Soviet forces at Kiev was sealed. Days later, the city of Kiev fell to the Germans, and an astonishing 665,000 men were taken into captivity, an experience that around 95 per cent would not survive. The Kiev debacle was just one of several major disasters to overcome the Soviets between June and December of 1941. Indeed, other encirclement operations before Kiev also netted huge volumes of prisoners – the fall of Bialystok-Minsk yielded 300,000 prisoners, and that of Smolensk 350,000 prisoners. It is estimated that the Soviets lost around three million troops during 1941 alone. ∎

Crewmen of a German reconnaissance vehicle take a break from the advance. The vast distances of the Russian territory took a severe toll on German vehicles, with as many being lost through mechanical failure as through combat.

PEARL HARBOR

FOR THE JAPANESE, PEARL HARBOR WAS A MASTERPIECE OF TACTICAL PLANNING IN THE NEW ART OF NAVAL AVIATION WARFARE.

For the United States, Pearl Harbor was an unparalleled military and maritime disaster.

WARNINGS IGNORED

Pearl Harbor, Hawaii, was the home of the US Navy's Pacific Fleet. The Japanese hoped that a pre-emptive air attack on this base would cripple the United States' naval capacity to resist Japanese expansion in the Pacific, especially as Japan's land operations were reliant on unhindered amphibious deployments. The attack was conceived by Admiral Isoroku Yamamoto (Commander in Chief, Imperial Japanese Navy). With warship and logistical support from the Japanese Kurile islands, he deployed a naval force of six aircraft carriers (containing 450 aircraft) to positions within 800km (500 miles) of Hawaii. The total journey was 5440km (3400 miles), and went undetected by the Americans, despite some intelligence warnings in November 1941 that Japan was planning an attack on Pearl Harbor. ➤➤

KEY FACTS

26 November 1941 – Japanese carrier forces set sail from the Kurile islands.

7 December 1941 – Japanese launch massive air assault against US Pacific Fleet at Pearl Harbor, sinking 16 US vessels in a two-hour attack.

Prior US intelligence regarding the attack not effectively handled or interpreted.

American shipping lies devastated at Pearl Harbor – although the Japanese did not cripple the US carrier fleet.

Above: The magazine of the destroyer USS Shaw *explodes with a huge blast after having been struck by bombs from Japanese dive-bombers.*

On 7 December 1941, the aircraft of the Japanese First Air Fleet began to take off from positions 443km (275 miles) north of Hawaii. Tragically, the US Opana Mobile Radar Unit detected the incoming flights about 200km (124 miles) from Pearl Harbor, but the personnel interpreted the signals as those from an expected flight of B-17s.

THE DEVASTATION BEGINS

At 0755, the attacks began on the 70 anchored US warships, a first wave of 180 Japanese dive-bombers and torpedo aircraft sinking 13 vessels, including two battleships. Two more waves added to the destruction, which finally ended at 0945. In total, six battleships, three destroyers, three light cruisers and four other ships were sunk, while 164 US aircraft were destroyed, most on the ground. A total of 2043 people, military and civilian, were killed – all for the loss of only 29 Japanese aircraft. It was a profound military disaster for the United States, one which could have been lessened by simple measures such as torpedo nets in the harbour. However, at the time of the attack, US carriers and heavy cruisers were at sea, and these provided the foundation for the subsequent US naval supremacy during the Pacific War. ■

A total of 164 US aircraft were destroyed on the ground in Japanese strafing and bomb attacks.

CRETE

**THE GERMAN INVASION OF CRETE IN MAY 1941 WAS A SUCCESS –
THE ISLAND WAS EVENTUALLY CAPTURED AND THE ALLIES EXPELLED.**

However, it was also in many ways an outright disaster for the
men who carried out the operation, the German *Fallschirmjäger*
paratroopers. The paratroopers had gained Hitler's respect during
blitzkrieg operations in Norway and the Low Countries in 1940,
and these were seen as the most viable way of capturing Crete.

UNDERMINED BY INTELLIGENCE

The operation planned for the deployment of 22,750 troops, either
para-dropped or air-landed in gliders. They were to be launched in
two waves against the northern coastline of Crete, capturing key
towns and airfields at Máleme, Canea, Suda Port, Rétimo and
Heráklion, before advancing southwards and squeezing the British
off the island. The British and Commonwealth forces on Crete –
numbering around 42,000 men – had been informed of the German plans through ULTRA code
interceptions. Although, their commander, Lieutenant General Freyberg, had not positioned his men
to best advantage on the island, the Germans would still be dropping over ready troops. The invasion
itself began on 20 May, thousands of German paras of the 7th Airborne Division blotting out the sky ➤

KEY FACTS

20 May 1941 – German
invasion of Crete, Operation
Mercur, begins with
massive airborne deployment
of parachute- and glider-
landed forces.

Allied defenders made aware
of forthcoming invasion by
ULTRA intelligence, and kill
3000 German troops on the
first day alone.

1 June 1941 – Crete finally falls
to the Germans, but at a cost
of 7000 dead, nearly two-
thirds of the invasion force.

German paratroopers prepare to embark aboard Junkers Ju-52 transport aircraft for the flight to Crete. The Ju-52 was a superb transporter, but proved very vulnerable to anti-aircraft fire in ground-assault roles.

over northern Crete. They dropped straight into blistering waves of small-arms fire, which killed hundreds in mid-air. Countless other troops injured themselves landing on Crete's rocky surface and were finished off at close quarters. Para weapons were dropped separately in canisters, and this meant that some Germans went into action with little more than a pistol.

AIRBORNE MASSACRE

The glider-borne soldiers fared little better – many of the slow-moving craft were shot down by AA fire. It was a mind-numbing slaughter – by the end of the first day, 3000 German soldiers were dead. Only on 21 May were the paras able to secure positions around some of the key objectives, as much down to Freyberg's misreading of further ULTRA intelligence as German combat performance. Subsequent reinforcements consolidated the German invasion, and Crete itself finally fell to the Germans on 1 June, with 18,000 Allied soldiers being taken as POWs. However, the total cost for German airborne forces was 7000 dead, about 60 per cent of the troops deployed. Such a cost was unacceptable. Hitler never again authorized a large-scale para operation, and the *Fallschirmjäger* spent the rest of the war as elite infantry. ■

Above: British officers make a reconnaissance tour of the island of Crete prior to the German invasion. It is a testimony to the fighting quality of the German paratroopers that the Allies, with forewarning of the invasion plans, were unable to prevent the final German victory.

Paratroopers advance across Crete. German paras were almost entirely defenceless during the para drop and initial landing, most of their small arms being contained in independently dropped weapons containers.

SINGAPORE

THE FALL OF SINGAPORE IN FEBRUARY 1942 STILL RANKS AS THE WORST DISASTER IN THE HISTORY OF THE BRITISH ARMY.

It was the culmination of the Japanese army's impressive Malayan campaign, which had begun on 8 December 1941.

PRESSED TO SURRENDER

British forces found themselves continually outflanked and outgunned, and were driven back down the Malayan peninsula. Kuala Lumpur fell on 11 January, and by the 20th British and Commonwealth troops began their withdrawal across the Johore Straits onto Singapore at Malaya's extreme south. The commander of the Singapore garrison was Lieutenant General Arthur Percival, who carved the island up into defensive sectors manned by a variety of British, Malayan, Australian and Indian formations. All Allied troops on the Malayan mainland had been evacuated to Singapore by 31 January, whereupon the bridge across the Johore Straits was demolished. A total of 85,000 Allied troops now awaited the Japanese onslaught. On 4 February, Percival rejected a Japanese request for British surrender, then, on the night of ➤➤

KEY FACTS

- **11 January 1942** – Singapore acts as the final retreat for 85,000 Allied troops pushed southwards by Japan's Malayan campaign.
- **Japanese landings** on Singapore begin on night of 8/9 February, the Japanese being specialists in night-time amphibious manoeuvres.
- **British resistance** finally collapses on 15 February, with 62,000 Allied troops being captured.

Japanese soldiers chalk up another victory. Tactically they outclassed the Allies in the first months of the Pacific War.

All prisoners were treated abysmally by their Japanese captors. Thousands were worked to death in construction projects throughout Southeast Asia, mainly in jungle clearance and rail laying.

8/9 February, units of the Japanese 5th and 18th divisions landed on Singapore's northwestern coast, elements of the Japanese Guards Division having made a feint attack against the northeastern coastline the night before. Soon Japanese engineers had repaired the Johore causeway, allowing the deployment of 30,000 troops of the Twenty-Fifth Army onto the island.

UNPRECEDENTED DEFEAT

The poorly positioned British and Commonwealth forces, stretched thinly around the coastline, were soon put into a southward retreat, constantly harassed by Japanese bombers and ground-attack aircraft (the Japanese had quickly achieved air superiority). By 12 February, most of the Allies were confined in a narrow perimeter around Singapore City. Singapore's civilian population was in a desperate panic, and the island's water supplies began to collapse through bomb-damaged pipework. Finally, on 15 February, Percival recognized that the situation was hopeless and surrendered to Lieutenant General Yamashita. The Japanese commander had expended 1714 dead and 3378 wounded to take Singapore. However, a total of 62,000 Allied soldiers fell into Japanese captivity. Winston Churchill described the catastrophe as 'the worst disaster and largest capitulation in British history'. ■

Singapore's civilian population attempts to flee from the Japanese advance. Just prior to the Japanese takeover, around 2000 civilians were being killed each day by Japanese air raids.

MIDWAY

IN MAY 1942, THE IMPERIAL JAPANESE NAVY CONCEIVED A PLAN TO CRUSH US CARRIER-BASED AIRPOWER IN THE PACIFIC THEATRE.

The plan was for a diversionary offensive against the Aleutian Islands to draw US naval assets north from around the island of Midway in the central Pacific. Next, a massive invasion force would take Midway and crush the remaining US fleet in a decisive open battle around the island.

SWIFT DESTRUCTION

The Japanese assembled almost the entire Japanese surface fleet for the Midway operation. Central to the action was the First Carrier Striking Force under Vice Admiral Nagumo, which contained Japan's four premier carriers – *Kaga*, *Akagi*, *Soryu* and *Hiryu*. Crucially, however, US intelligence intercepts around 22 May revealed the Midway operation, and Admiral Nimitz (Commander in Chief Pacific Fleet) assembled his naval forces into two carrier groups – Task Force 16 containing the carriers *Hornet* and *Enterprise*, and Task Force 17 with the USS *Yorktown* at the centre. Nimitz's focal targets were Nagumo's carriers. ➤➤

The Douglas SBD Dauntless was a two-seat carrierborne dive-bomber. It was a war-winning weapon in the Pacific, and sank more tons of Japanese shipping than any other US aircraft.

While the Japanese occupation of the Aleutians commenced on 3 June, the naval clash around Midway began the next day. Nagumo's aircraft made strikes against Midway island, but the vice admiral at this stage had no solid idea of the location of the US carriers. However, the Japanese fighter aircraft made short work of both an attack by US land-based aircraft flying from Midway and two subsequent attacks by carrier-based torpedo aircraft.

CARRIER LOSSES

At around 1000, all Japanese aircraft had returned to their carriers and were cramming the decks for refuelling and rearming. It was in this condition that a strike force of naval attack aircraft found the Japanese carriers. Bombs were dropped onto the crowded flight decks, creating enormous fuel and munitions explosions. Incredibly, it took only five minutes for the Japanese carriers *Kaga*, *Soryu* and *Akagi* to be destroyed. The *Hiryu* escaped to cripple the US carrier *Yorktown*, but was critically damaged later in the day by a strike from the USS *Enterprise*. She was scuttled the next day. With the carriers lost, the Japanese Midway operation collapsed, and the USA effectively gained control of the Pacific. ∎

A Japanese 'Mogami' class cruiser burns out of control after being hit by US dive-bombers. After Midway the Japanese lost effective control of the Pacific waters.

The remote military base of Midway island burns after a Japanese air attack.

DIEPPE

THE AMPHIBIOUS RAID ON THE GERMAN-OCCUPIED FRENCH PORT OF DIEPPE, OPERATION JUBILEE, WAS LAUNCHED ON 19 AUGUST 1942.

The operation's objective was to land a force of 4963 Canadians, 1075 British and 50 US Ranger soldiers at or around Dieppe, seize the port, hold it for around 12 hours to gather intelligence, then re-embark the landing ships. The total naval contingent for the raid was 237 vessels.

DEFENDERS PREPARED, ATTACKS DELAYED

The operation was meant to begin at 0450 with flanking attacks against significant coastal defences. Critically, however, the defenders were forewarned after a German convoy saw, and engaged, the invasion fleet at 0348. At Berneval, only six boats of No. 3 Commando soldiers put ashore half an hour late, taking major casualties from clifftop machine-gun positions. At Puys, soldiers of the Royal Regiment of Canada were also landed late and straight into German machine-gun fire – 211 men had been killed by 0830. The Pourville troops went ashore in the wrong ➤➤

Allied prisoners are marched away to captivity after the disastrous raid at Dieppe. Nearly 2500 soldiers were taken into captivity, providing an enormous propaganda victory for the Germans.

Wehrmacht infantry stand amid the equipment and bodies of the Allied defeat at Dieppe, scattered around the interior of a landing craft.

position and were forced to abandon their attack at 1000 hours, leaving behind around 150 dead and 541 captured. Only No. 4 Commando at Varengville had reasonable success, capturing all its gun-battery objectives.

IMPOSSIBLE ODDS

At 0520, the main Allied assault went in, which simply compounded the emerging disaster. Only 15 of 29 Churchill tanks deployed made it across the beach, and these were stuck behind German anti-tank barriers while the infantry were being slaughtered in their hundreds. At 1050, Major General John Hamilton Roberts, commander of the Canadian troops, ordered a withdrawal. Dieppe cost the lives of 1027 Allied soldiers, with another 2340 being captured. Such a great cost cannot, unfortunately, be balanced against any clear tactical or strategic gains. ■

Allied soldiers aboard a landing craft heading for Dieppe. A typical British landing craft at this stage of the war could hold around 60 fully equipped troops and two or three medium tanks.

STALINGRAD

THE GERMAN ASSAULT ON STALINGRAD IN 1942 WAS PART OF HITLER'S SPRING CAMPAIGN AGAINST THE CAUCASUS.

Following the launch of the offensive on 28 June, the Sixth Army under General Paulus reached the river Volga on 23 August, and forced three Soviet armies back into the city.

VICTORY DENIED

Through hideously costly close combat, the 200,000 men of the Sixth Army, supported by the Fourth Panzer Army, steadily drove the Russians back through the city. By mid-November, the Soviets held a sliver of territory barely 15km (6 miles) long and (at its thickest) 1.6km (1 mile) deep on the Volga's west bank, which Stalin held by pouring in hundreds of thousands of troops. Disease, combat and cold-related injuries devastated the German ranks, yet, for the Sixth Army, worse was to come.

On 19 November a massive Russian encirclement operation was launched north and south of Stalingrad, the pincers closing shut around Kalach on 23 November. Hitler, acting on Göring's vain assurances that the Luftwaffe could maintain the Sixth Army by air ➤➤

KEY FACTS

August 1942 – German Sixth Army and Fourth Panzer Army attack Stalingrad.

19 November – Soviets launch massive counteroffensive, encircling Stalingrad on 23 November.

2 February 1943 – surviving German forces surrender, the Germans having suffered 100,000 dead.

A German unit mans an MG34 machine gun to create a defensive position in the ruins of Stalingrad.

➤➤

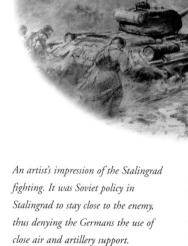

An artist's impression of the Stalingrad fighting. It was Soviet policy in Stalingrad to stay close to the enemy, thus denying the Germans the use of close air and artillery support.

supplies, refused a German break-out. A relief operation launched by Manstein on 12 December was halted short of Stalingrad by the 23rd, and the Luftwaffe rarely managed to exceed 80 tons (88 tonnes) of supplies each day. In Stalingrad, the Sixth Army bled, froze and starved.

DEATH OF AN ARMY

On 10 January, a huge Soviet assault in the city began to crush the surviving Germans, and on the 25th the Germans lost control of their last airstrip. Between 31 January and 2 February 1943, the Sixth Army surrendered. More than 100,000 Germans had been killed and another 100,000 entered captivity – only 5000 survived to return home. The defeat at Stalingrad crushed the myth of German invincibility. Now the Germans would be fighting, and losing, a defensive war. ∎

A Russian field gun unit fires from within the twisted landscape of a bombed-out factory.

KURSK

The battle of Kursk hammered the final nail into the German coffin on the Eastern Front.

During the winter of 1942/43, Soviet advances had created a massive territorial bulge around Kursk, occupied by the might of two Soviet fronts, the Central Front and Voronezh Front, with six armies of the Stavka Front held in reserve.

Strong resistance

Hitler ordered an operation to pinch out this salient using the Ninth Army (General Model) from the north and the Fourth Panzer Army (General Hoth) and Operational Group Kempf (Lieutenant General Wehrner Kempf) from the south. Total forces amassed around Kursk were enormous, the Germans having 700,000 soldiers, 2400 tanks/assault guns and 1800 aircraft. The Soviet opposition was even greater, however, with 1.3 million soldiers, 3400 tanks/assault guns and 2100 aircraft. Furthermore, Allied intelligence had already betrayed Operation Citadel, so the Soviets were waiting to fight what became the largest land battle in history. ➤➤

KEY FACTS

- **5 July 1943** – the Germans launch Operation Citadel, an attempt to destroy the Soviet salient around Kursk.
- **Massive Soviet** resistance results in the largest land battle in history, with all main German advances stopped by 12 July.
- **23 July** – German forces are pushed back beyond their start lines, with enormous losses in men and armour.

A column of Tiger tanks heads forwards to the battlefield of Kursk. The Tiger was a superb combat tank, although on the Eastern Front it was prone to mechanical failure, particularly in its wheel suspension.

A German unit takes a break from operations. By 1943 the Germans were facing an enemy of greater tactical sophistication than they encountered in 1941, and with huge resources of manpower and weaponry which German industry could not match.

Citadel was launched on 5 July 1943. Model's advance to the north soon met trouble. Pre-prepared Soviet defensive lines and reinforcements from the Second Tank Army meant that the Ninth Army made a slow advance, at the cost of too many casualties. An advance of only 10km (6 miles) cost 200 tanks, 200 aircraft and 25,000 dead, and by 9 July the German's northern thrust had stalled.

NO GAINS

In the south, meanwhile, Hoth and Kempf made better progress, partly because Hoth's unit contained the excellent 2nd SS and 48th Panzer Corps and also because his attack had achieved some operational surprise. Hoth's Panzers pushed a wedge 40km (25 miles) deep into the Voronezh Front, but eventually became embroiled in a tank battle, with casualties increasing to 350 tanks destroyed and 10,000 men killed. Hoth, too, was stopped.

On 12 July, coinciding with Allied landings on Sicily, the Soviets went on the offensive, and Hitler scrapped Citadel the next day. By the 23rd, the Soviets had retaken all ground lost, and the Germans had suffered more than 58,000 dead, plus around 700 tanks destroyed. For no gains whatsoever, the Germans had sacrificed more than they could afford. ∎

Wehrmacht troops scan the horizon for signs of Soviet activity. Soviet losses in men and materiel at Kursk were actually higher than the Germans', but they could better absorb such losses than the German army.

BYELORUSSIA

OPERATION BAGRATION, THE SOVIET OFFENSIVE TO CLEAR OUT THE GERMANS FROM BYELORUSSIA AND PUSH ON INTO THE REICH ITSELF, WAS ONE OF MANY DISASTERS THAT OVERCAME THE DISINTEGRATING GERMAN ARMY IN 1944.

By June 1944, the German frontline in the east stretched from the Gulf of Finland down to Odessa on the Black Sea, with a large salient in Byelorussia occupied by the German Army Group Centre under Field Marshal Ernst von Busch.

OVERWHELMING FORCE

Against this salient, the Russians planned Operation Bagration. Devised in May 1944, this envisaged breakthroughs all along the front, with three Soviet Byelorussian fronts trapping and destroying the bulk of Army Group Centre forces around Minsk. By mid-June, the Germans had learned of the operation, and bulked up frontline strength to 1.2 million men, 9500 guns/mortars, 900 tanks/assault guns and 1350 aircraft. Impressive figures, but they paled in comparison to the Soviet forces – 1.4 million men, 31,000 guns/mortars, 5200 tanks/assault guns and 5000 aircraft. ➤➤

KEY FACTS

22 June 1944 – Soviet forces launch Operation Bagration, a massive campaign to eject the Germans from Byelorussia and destroy Army Group Centre.

11 July – three entire German armies have been surrounded and crushed. The Germans are ejected from Russian soil with the loss of more than 200,000 troops and huge amounts of armour.

Cavalry were ideal troops for patrolling and reconnaisance in the vast spaces of the Ukraine and Byelorussia. Men and horses were independent of an army moving on tracks or wheels and were capable of shocking ill-equipped troops.

With Operation Bagration, huge numbers of Soviet citizens were liberated from Nazi governance. However, almost everything they owned had been destroyed, and they were left to rebuild shattered lives, often under Soviet suspicion as potential collaborationists.

Between 19 and 21 June, Russian partisans prepared for Operation Bagration by exploding over 40,000 demolitions charges along railway lines, roads and communications systems, which meant that German logistics were severely hampered when the final offensive was launched at 0400 on 22 June. Army Group Centre – 37 divisions scattered along 1287km (800 miles) of front – was completely overwhelmed by 166 divisions of Soviet troops.

DOWNFALL

By 11 July, the German Third Panzer, Fourth and Ninth armies had been encircled and crushed. In the first week of Operation Bagration alone, German forces lost 200,000 men and most of their armour, cataclysmic losses among an already weakened army. For Army Group Centre, its own losses included 17 divisions entirely destroyed, with another 50 divisions experiencing a 50 per cent reduction in strength. Stalin even had 57,000 German prisoners paraded through the streets of Moscow on 17 July. The disaster had been exacerbated by Hitler's typical refusal to allow tactical withdrawals. German forces were routed along the length of the front, and by the end of August Soviet forces were pushing into the Reich territory of East Prussia. ∎

The war on the Eastern Front took a terrible toll on civilian lives and property. The Soviet Army would begin to exact its vengeance as it pushed into East Prussia in early 1945, with an estimated 1 million Germans dying in the refugee crisis.

WARSAW UPRISING

IN JULY 1944, WITH THE GERMAN ARMY IN RETREAT ON ALL FRONTS, THE COMMANDER IN CHIEF OF THE POLISH HOME ARMY, LIEUTENANT GENERAL TADEUSZ KOMOROWSKI, DEVELOPED PLANS FOR AN UPRISING AGAINST THE GERMAN OCCUPIERS IN WARSAW.

The uprising's aims were as much political as military. By expelling the Germans in advance of the Soviet arrival, the Poles hoped to ensure a home government, which would prohibit a Soviet political takeover. This aim was to be at the root of the tragedy that followed.

POLITICAL SACRIFICE

The uprising began on 1 August 1944, with General Antoni Chrusciel in command. Chrusciel had around 38,000 troops at his disposal, backed by total civilian support, against a German garrison of 22,000 men. However, the insurgents were very lightly armed, only 14 per cent of troops actually having firearms, and there were some 90,000 German troops available in outlying districts. Much of the city was taken back into Polish hands over the first two weeks, whereupon the strategy shifted to the defensive, with Komorowski hoping to hold on until British/US ➤➤

KEY FACTS

1 August 1944 – Polish Home Army in Warsaw begins an uprising against German occupation, retaking much of the city.

25 August – German SS-led counterattack is unleashed, which forces the surrender of the Poles on 1 October.

More than a quarter of a million Poles are killed in the uprising, with a further 550,000 transported out to the concentration camps.

A German rifle salute is fired over the graves of soldiers killed during the Warsaw Uprising. The brutal German supression of the uprising made no distinction between civilian and military personnel.

➤➤

The Warsaw population built crude defences around the city during the rising, but they were unable to prevent the German annihilation of the city.

support or Soviet advances secured the situation. It was not to be, and Himmler furiously ordered SS Obergruppenführer Erich von dem Bach-Zelewski to retake the city. He did this with some 22,000 well-armed German troops, which included the insidious Police Brigade, made up of criminals and Soviet deserters, under Oberführer Oskar Dirlwanger.

LEFT TO DIE

The Germans were given a free hand to slaughter all Poles, 40,000 being killed in the first two weeks of German action. A huge German counterattack from 25 August steadily snuffed out the Polish resistance in brutal house-to-house fighting. Tragically, by this time the Soviet army was actually on Warsaw's eastern suburbs, but evidence suggests that Stalin stopped his advance so that the Polish resistance would be destroyed, therefore facilitating an easy political handover to the Soviets. He even refused US and British aircraft the use of airfields to land supplies for the Poles. Komoroski surrendered his forces on 1 October after 15,000 Polish soldiers and up to 250,000 civilians had been killed and over 90 per cent of the city destroyed. ■

SS Gruppenführer Heinz Reinefahrt conducts a planning meeting with his staff at his command post at Wola during the initial days of the Warsaw Uprising, when the Germans were struggling to control the situation.

ARNHEM

OPERATION MARKET GARDEN WAS FIELD MARSHAL MONTGOMERY'S PLAN TO USE US AND BRITISH AIRBORNE FORCES TO CAPTURE A SERIES OF BRIDGES BETWEEN THE BELGIAN BORDER AND THE DUTCH TOWN OF ARNHEM.

With the bridges secured, the idea was that the British XXX Corps could then drive northwards along a secure corridor and force a crossing of the Rhine into Germany before winter set in.

ISOLATED AND OUTNUMBERED

Market Garden was launched on 17 September 1944, with some 16,500 airborne troops being para-dropped and a further 3500 landing in gliders. Surprise was achieved, and the US operations made headway. Zon, Veghel and Grave were taken on the 17th, and Nijmegen fell on the 20th to a joint attack by US paratroops and the advancing British XXX Corps. At Arnhem, however, the most northerly objective, the British were dropped 11km (7 miles) from their target, and faced a costly four-hour fight into the town (unknown to the Allies was the fact that the 9th and 10 SS Panzer divisions were refitting in the area). Radio communications failed, ➤➤

KEY FACTS

17 September 1944 – Operation Market Garden is launched.

Allied intelligence had massively underestimated German strength in the Arnhem area.

British XXX Corps unable to rescue the British paras at Arnhem, and nearly 8000 troops are lost.

Arnhem was Montgomery's attempt to force an early crossing of the river Rhine into Germany. After its chronic failure, the Allied commander never quite regained his reputation, especially among the Americans.

German soldiers open fire on the Allied paratroopers. As with the Germans in Crete in 1941, the Arnhem operation taught the Allies that large-scale unilateral airborne operation carried unacceptably high rates of loss.

and only 2nd Parachute Battalion troops actually reached Arnhem's road bridge (the rail bridge had already been blown), whereupon they were steadily decimated by German armour. The rest of the British around Arnhem were isolated and outnumbered, and Polish reinforcements were unable to fight their way through.

HEAVY LOSSES

Market Garden was an unravelling disaster. Owing to heavy German resistance and the tardiness of XXX Corps, the British overland advance ground to a halt just north of Nijmegen. The British paras holding the Arnhem bridge had now been driven from the bridge and fought for survival in the town until 26 September. By that date, some 2200 Allied soldiers had escaped, but some 7600 troops were killed or taken prisoner. To compound the failure, US troops suffered 3532 casualties during the subsequent eight weeks of holding the line. ∎

British paratroopers advance in northern Europe. Britain's parachute formations were created following the German successes with airborne deployments in Belgium, Norway and Holland in 1940.

KOREA

THE US MILITARY'S POST-WAR COMBAT CAREER BEGAN WITH TWO DISASTERS, BOTH IN KOREA AND BOTH IN 1950.

On 25 June 1950, the North Korean communist Korean People's Army (KPA) crossed the 38th parallel and invaded the US-supported South Korea.

PSYCHED OUT

Facing them was the ill-prepared and corrupt Republic of Korea (RoK) army and a mixture of US army units, including many new conscripts pulled in from easy occupation duties in Japan. The USA initially underestimated the power of the threat – President Truman referred to the US response as a 'police action' – but it soon became apparent that the North Korean juggernaut would not be stopped by the ill-equipped US troops, who were hampered by chronic deficiencies in winter clothing, ammunition and vehicles. Entire US divisions were routed, many losing around 30 per cent casualties, and in only two months US and RoK forces were squeezed back into a small pocket of territory around Pusan on the southeast coast. There the line was finally held. Even ➤➤

KEY FACTS

25 June 1950 – North Korea invades South Korea, and drives a combined US/RoK army back to around the port of Pusan.

Inchon landing and subsequent UN offensive pushes KPA back to the borders of China.

China enters the war on 25 October, and pushes the US/UN army back over the 38th parallel.

In the sub-zero conditions of a Korean winter, US troops stand back to watch a napalm strike on an enemy position.

better, General Douglas MacArthur's daring landing at Inchon behind KPA lines on 15 September enabled a reversal of the situation, and a US/UN force (with troops contributed from 17 other UN nations) managed to push the KPA back over the 38th parallel, into the North, and right up to the border with China. China's response was to pouring over 130,000 of its own troops into North Korea around 25 October.

US troops fire a recoilless rifle against communist forces. The UN enjoyed a total superiority in equipment over the Koreans and Chinese, but for much of the war their troops suffered from low morale, poor training and a general willingness to retreat.

CHINESE INVASION

The US/UN army now collapsed a second time. Despite having complete superiority in air power, artillery, infantry arms and armour, the army panicked and was forced into retreat. Such was the psychological fear of the Chinese masses that soldiers reported 'bug out fever' – just the hint of Chinese soldiers in the area sent entire units into rapid retreat. Heavy fighting also slashed the ranks of US manpower, as did the Korean winter, with temperatures of –20°C (–4°F). US and UN forces were consequently pushed back over the 38th parallel, and the South Korean capital, Seoul, fell for the second time on 4 January. It was a calamitous performance for an army fresh from victory in the Pacific and Europe. ■

The US amphibious landings at Inchon in September 1950 enabled UN forces to push the North Koreans out of South Korea. However, Chinese intervention in the war in October precipitated a second US/UN rout.

DIEN BIEN PHU

IN LATE 1953, THE FRENCH IN INDOCHINA WERE SEEKING A MILITARY MEANS TO END WAR WITH THE COMMUNIST VIET MINH.

General Henri Navarre (Commander in Chief in Indochina from May 1953) came up with a daring strategy. In an attempt to interdict the Viet Minh's Laotian invasion and supply lines, he decided to deploy a large airborne force near the village of Dien Bien Phu, on a wide plain approx 19km (12 miles) long by 13km (8 miles) wide, and ringed by the T'ai mountains. His men would be entirely surrounded, with resupply coming only from the air, but the intention was to draw the Viet Minh into a crushing conventional defeat.

FIERCE RESISTANCE
Parachute deployment of Airborne Battle Group I began on 20 November 1953. The French transformed Dien Bien Phu into a geographic fortress, with eight heavily armed strongpoints and a garrison strength of 10,800 men supported by artillery, 10 M24 light tanks and six on-station Bearcat fighter-bombers. However, the legendary Viet Minh general Vo Ngyuen Giap deployed five ➤➤

French paratroopers carry away one of the many troops injured by almost constant Viet Minh shellfire.

Viet Minh soldiers make a human wave assault against French positions. As the USA would find out in the subsequent Vietnam War, the death of a Viet Minh soldier had negligible political consequences when compared to the death of a French or US soldier.

divisions of troops around the plain, and against French predictions his soldiers manhandled 300 105mm artillery pieces up onto the mountains. The siege had begun.

SHRINKING PERIMETER

Artillery fire began to pound the French on 31 January 1954, while Viet Minh anti-aircraft fire reduced air supply by 30 per cent. Ferocious French resistance meant that by 4 April Giap had lost 2000 men. Yet despite air-dropped reinforcements, the French perimeter had shrunk to little more than 600m (1 mile) in diameter. Switching tactics, Giap steadily sapped his men – now more than 50,000 strong – forward in trenches. The strongpoints collapsed one by one and a final attack forced the French surrender on 7 May. French losses were 7184 men dead, and 12,000 troops captured. Giap had lost 20,000 men, but the French finally gave up their Indochina colony in 1954 at the Geneva Accords. ■

As the siege developed, Dien Bien Phu began to resemble the trench systems of the Western Front in World War I.

SIX-DAY WAR

THERE IS NO DENYING THAT THE SIX-DAY WAR OF 1967 FULLY
DEMONSTRATED THE BRILLIANCE OF THE ISRAELI WAR MACHINE.

However, the gravity of the Arab collapse should not be
underestimated, the six-day conflict ranking as one of the greatest
defeats of post-World War II military history.

MODERN BLITZKRIEG

The conflict was precipitated by a dramatic escalation of tension
between Israel and her surrounding Arab neighbours in 1966/67.
Egypt deployed up to seven divisions of troops in Sinai, previously
occupied by UN troops as buffer security for Israel's western
border, and naval units also blockaded the Straits of Tiran.

Simultaneously, the Arab nations announced that they would be forming a unified military command.
Suddenly Israel looked to be in a stranglehold, and by 20 May she had mobilized all her forces for
offensive operations. The Arab forces were confident of their dominance over Israel. Israel had
264,000 men, 800 tanks and 350 aircraft, whereas the three principal Arab protagonists – Egypt, Syria
and Jordan – had combined forces of 340,000 men, 1800 tanks and 610 aircraft. Most of the Arab
equipment and tactical thinking was Soviet in origin. What would become swiftly apparent, however,
was that the Israeli forces were utterly superior in terms of both equipment and the quality of their ➤➤

On the road through the Mitla Pass, destroyed Egyptian transport vehicles litter the roadside, victims of strikes by Israeli Defence Force aircraft. Air power was the decisive factor in the Six-Day War, although there remained heavy ground fighting.

Above: Although the Six-Day War tends to be identified with the air campaign and desert fighting, the war was fought in a variety of terrains. Bitter mountain warfare was conducted in the Golan Heights, and street fighting occured in the streets of Jerusalem, seen here.

soldiers. On 5 June 1967, at 0845 Egyptian time, Israel launched an awesome rolling air attack against ground targets throughout Sinai and Egypt.

RUTHLESS DOMINATION

At the time of the attack most of the Egyptian air force was stood down, and it was massacred on the ground. In one day 300 Egyptian aircraft were destroyed; the Jordanian and Syrian air forces were similarly massacred by the end of the day. Without air cover, the Egyptian troops in Sinai could not contain the huge three-pronged Israeli armoured thrust, which used Centurion tanks with double the killing range of the Egyptian T54/55s. Despite occasional heavy resistance, Egypt collapsed, and by 8 June the Israelis had secured territory up to the Gulf of Suez. To the east, Jordan lost the West Bank with more than 6000 casualties. In the north the Syrians were unable to hold on to the Golan Heights, despite their superior defensive positions, losing 250 tanks and 200 artillery pieces in their defeat. By 11 June, the Arab collapse was complete, and Israel had extended her territory with Sinai, the West Bank of the river Jordan (including Jerusalem) and the Golan Heights. Israel's brilliant campaign had cost her 3252 casualties, while Arab casualty estimates reached more than 40,000. ■

Israeli Centurion V tanks head into battle. The Centurion's gun had almost double the killing range of Egyptian T55s.

OPERATION EAGLE CLAW

OPERATION EAGLE CLAW WAS A RESPONSE TO THE OCCUPATION OF THE US EMBASSY IN TEHERAN, IRAN. ON 4 NOVEMBER 1979, REVOLUTIONARIES HAD TAKEN 53 OCCUPANTS HOSTAGE.

Protracted negotiations came to nothing, so six months later the US government opted for military action.

BAD PLANNING, BAD LUCK

Eagle Claw was an elaborate plan. First, a Delta Force team would be flown aboard three C-130 transport aircraft to the remote Dasht-e-Karir desert (known to the Americans as 'Desert One'), roughly 500km (310 miles) southeast of Teheran. They would be accompanied by three C-130 refuelling aircraft, for refuelling eight US Navy RH-53D helicopters that would land at Desert One from the USS *Nimitz* stationed in the Persian Gulf. The helicopters would then take an assault team out to a hiding location only 8km (5 miles) from Teheran. The next day, a Delta Force assault team would drive into the city aboard six Mercedes trucks (supplied by an agent) and make the hostage rescue, then call in the helicopters to rescue them from the embassy roof or a nearby football stadium. From there, they would be flown to Manzarieh airfield to the south, which would have been seized ➤➤

KEY FACTS

24 April 1980 – Operation Eagle Claw is launched, the attempt to rescue 53 hostages from US Embassy and foreign office in Teheran.

Delta Force troops deployed to Desert One location by six C-130s.

Eight US Navy RH-38D helicopters head for Desert One. Two abort mid-flight owing to mechanical failure. Another helicopter hits a C-130 at Desert One; the resulting explosion kills eight aviators. Eagle Claw is called off.

A C-130 aircraft delivers a refuelling mission to an RH-53D helicopter. The C-130 is one of the post-war world's most successful aircraft, having first flown in 1954 and subsequently been produced in variants ranging from reconnaissance aircraft to gunship.

Carrier forces have been crucial to the US operational presence in the Middle East region. Although the Eagle Claw operation was a failure, subsequent US Navy operations in the region have been stunning successes, particularly in the wars against Iraq.

by US Rangers, then flown out on C-141 transports. When the operation was finally launched on 24 April 1980, it initially appeared to go to plan.

MISSION FAILURE

The Delta Force soldiers were transported to Desert One without hindrance. At the site, the soldiers had to interdict traffic on a nearby road, first detaining 45 people who had been passing on a bus, then destroying a petrol tanker with an anti-tank rocket. Meanwhile, the eight US Navy helicopters were on their way. However, two helicopters were forced to abort, owing to mechanical failure, and the rest flew into huge dust storms, forcing two helicopters to land temporarily.

Chronically behind schedule, and with two helicopters down, the mission was aborted at Desert One. Yet tragedy struck when a RH-53D crashed into a C-130 on the ground, producing a mixed fuel/ammunition explosion that killed eight aviation crew (five on the C-130; three on the RH-38D). The remaining personnel were then flown to Oman aboard the remaining C-130s. The critical failure of Operation Eagle Claw was a terrible combat initiation for the newly created US Delta Force team. The hostages were finally released 444 days after capture. ∎

RH-53D helicopters, here seen painted in desert colours on the deck of a US carrier. A typical RH-53 helicopter has a crew of six (two pilots, four other crew) and can carry around 14,545kg (32,000lb) of cargo.

BRAVO TWO ZERO

THE BRITISH SPECIAL AIR SERVICE (SAS) IS NOT IMMUNE TO AMATEURISM AND DISASTER.

On 22 January 1991, during the First Gulf War, an eight-man SAS patrol codenamed 'Bravo Two Zero' was deployed under cover of darkness by Chinook helicopter into western Iraq. The unit's mission was to spend two weeks observing a major road through the region – known as the Main Supply Route (MSR) – and noting the traffic, particularly deployment of mobile SCUD missile launchers. The team went in badly prepared, dressed only in lightweight summer clothing despite the potential harshness of the Iraqi winter. Intelligence was scanty, and each man was carrying around 54kg (120lb) of kit.

UNABLE TO COMMUNICATE

First light soon revealed deficiencies in intelligence – the area was far more populated with both military installations and civilian traffic than estimated, including an Iraqi anti-aircraft position only 200m (656ft) from the team's lying-up position in a dried-up wadi. The men realized they had to be extracted, but they had earlier been given incorrect radio frequencies and were unable to contact rescue helicopters. They decided to wait for helicopter pickup according to ➤➤

The now infamous Bravo Two Zero team, here seen about to set out on their fateful mission into Iraq.

The crest of the SAS, which bears the legendary motto 'Who Dares Wins'. The dagger in the centre of the badge is meant to be the sword Excalibur., symbolizing truth and justice. Credit for the design of the badge goes to Bob Tait, a soldier in the SAS in 1941.

lost-comms procedures, but were spotted by a small boy, who immediately alerted nearby troops. Bravo Two Zero decided they had to move, and became involved in firefights with Iraqi troops.

ATTRITION

With Iraqi forces mobilizing, the team decided to head for the Syrian border 120km (75 miles) away, following the Euphrates River. Freezing winter weather now descended upon the team, and in blizzard conditions the team became separated into two groups. One group, which included SAS trouper Chris Ryan, lost a man through hypothermia, and later another soldier was captured by the Iraqis after attempting to obtain a vehicle. Chris Ryan made it to safety, having walked 300km (186 miles) in just over a week. The other group had a similar harrowing march, and hijacked an Iraqi taxi in an attempt to drive over the border. The attempt failed at a checkpoint, and a firefight only 7km (4 miles) from the Syrian border resulted in one man shot dead, another dying of hypothermia after swimming the Euphrates, and the other two men captured, including Andy McNab. All four captured men were tortured, but survived to be released at the end of the war. The mission was a complete and costly failure, resulting in three dead and four captured out of only eight men. ■

The Chinook helicopter has long been the workhorse of armies around the world. The SAS has frequently relied upon the Chinook for combat deployments, as despite its substantial size it still retains good low-altitude manoeuvrability.

MOGADISHU

Operation Irene was the now infamous attempt by US Special Forces to capture militia leaders loyal to Somali warlord Mohamed Farrah Aidid in Mogadishu in 1993.

US forces had first deployed to Somalia in 1992 as part of Operation Restore Hope, an attempt to control the country's factional violence and implement a coordinated relief effort.

Plan thwarted

Aidid soon became a hot target, his terrorist violence having cost the lives of 24 UN Pakistani troops and four US soldiers prior to the launch of Operation Irene on 3 October 1993. The plan was for a combined US Special Forces team, mainly US Rangers and Delta Force troops, to make a rappelling attack from hovering UH-60 Blackhawk helicopters onto a building where key militia personnel were meant to be in a meeting. After capturing them, the troops would transfer them to a US ground convoy which – according to the plan – would have travelled through the streets of Mogadishu to arrive at the destination five minutes after the air operation had gone in. ➡

KEY FACTS

- **3 October 1993** – Operation Irene begins. US Special Forces are deployed into Mogadishu to capture key militia personnel.
- **Two Blackhawk** helicopters are shot down and a force of US Rangers are trapped overnight in the city under constant attack.
- **4 October** – Surviving US troops are finally rescued, having suffered 18 dead and 79 wounded.

The American experience in Somalia in 1993 fundamentally changed the US military's approach to urban operations, and led to a far more cautious approach in deploying helicopters over densely populated, hostile areas.

Operation Irene unravelled immediately. Militia forces managed to down two Blackhawks with rocket-propelled grenades (RPGs), and the ground convoy was stopped by enemy street barricades. Soon several thousand militia and Somali civilians were firing upon the US troops, with 90 US Rangers pinned down around the first Blackhawk crash site, while two Delta Force soldiers were killed trying to protect the injured pilot at the second crash site (the pilot was taken hostage).

A LONG NIGHT

The Rangers spent the night under blistering fire, repeatedly battling off huge numbers of attackers, their situation made increasingly desperate by the lack of a US contingency plan. Only the next day did relief forces reach them, in the form of Malaysian and Pakistani UN units and troops from the US 10th Mountain Division. By the time the US troops were taken out to safety, 18 were dead and 79 wounded. An estimated 800 militia and Somali civilians were killed during the gun battles, which did demonstrate the superiority of the US soldiers. Nonetheless, urban warfare training consequently took higher priority in the US military. ∎

Above: One of the greatest problems of military operations in developing countries is a lack of easy distinction between combatants and non combatants. In African conflicts, children as young as eight have actively participated in guerrilla warfare, turning target selection for peacekeeping troops into ethical minefields.

An American soldier runs for cover during street-fighting operations. New technologies are entering service with the US Army that allow soldiers to have real-time computerized images of the battlefield presented on chest-mounted laptop computers.

INDEX